Memories
of His Mercy

RECOLLECTIONS OF THE
Grace and Providence of God

V. REV. PETER GILLQUIST

compiled and edited by Ginny Nieuwsma

ANCIENT FAITH
PUBLISHING
Chesterton, IN

Published by:
  Ancient Faith Publishing
  A Division of Ancient Faith Ministries
  P.O. Box 748
  Chesterton, IN 46304

All Old Testament quotations, unless otherwise identified, are from the Orthodox Study Bible, © 2008 by St. Athanasius Academy of Orthodox Theology (published by Thomas Nelson, Inc., Nashville, Tennessee) and are used by permission. New Testament quotations are from the New King James Version of the Bible, © 1982 by Thomas Nelson, Inc., and are used by permission.

ISBN: 978-1-944967-22-2

Printed in the United States of America

Contents

Only take heed to yourself, and diligently keep yourself, lest you forget the things your eyes have seen, and lest they depart from your heart all the days of your life. And teach them to your children and your grandchildren. (Deut. 4:9 NKJV)

Foreword

by Fr. Jon Braun

*By faith Abraham obeyed when he was called to
go out to the place which he would receive as an
inheritance. And he went out, not knowing
where he was going. (Heb. 11:8)*

My fifty-three–year friendship with Fr. Peter Gillquist began
in an unlikely place—in the high-jump pit at the University
of Minnesota in 1958. I didn't know Pete and he didn't know me,
but we competed against each other in an open track meet. Neither one of us won that meet, but I know for sure that he beat me.

A year later, a mutual friend formally introduced me to Fr.
Peter. We both had joined the staff of the Protestant Christian
ministry, Campus Crusade for Christ, on exactly the same day.
Oddly enough, we left that organization eight years later on
exactly the same day, and for all of our lives, our paths would
intersect in both remarkable and mundane ways. Our friendship
would endure up until the day of his repose on July 1, 2012.

Fr. Peter was a visionary. As young men working together in
outreach to college students, we did some brave and crazy things
at his initiative. One day I was visiting him when he was living in
Illinois and he said, "Let's go up to Eau Claire, Wisconsin, and see

what we can do." So we drove up to the University of Wisconsin Eau Claire, arriving on the campus at about twelve-fifteen, just after lunch. In the hours between twelve-fifteen and ten o'clock that night, we had gained permission to be on campus, we had visited a couple of the athletic teams to speak to them about Christ, we had visited several fraternities and sororities, and at nine o'clock at night we presented the gospel to about 550 collegians who showed up to hear us.

That was Fr. Peter. He made things happen. Once, he arranged one of the first Protestant meetings on the campus of the University of Notre Dame. He set up the whole presentation, lined up a musical group, and brought me in to speak. An unprecedented three thousand students turned out for that gospel meeting.

One late afternoon when he and I were in Knoxville at the University of Tennessee, we had an opening in our ministry schedule. Fr. Peter said, "Let's go over to the Sigma Alpha Epsilon (SAE) fraternity house and see if we can speak to them at dinner." We were going to line up a speaking engagement within the hour, at a frat house? Impossible! Nevertheless, we walked over to the SAE house. Since Fr. Peter happened to be an SAE, he said to the guys, "You know, we speak in fraternities and sororities all over America, and we're here tonight and we just happened to have a night free. Would you like us to speak to your fraternity? Invite us to dinner and we'll speak afterwards." It turned out to be an incredible meeting. Father Peter was always able to arrange the most unimaginable circumstances; to this day, he is at the center of some of my most unforgettable memories.

When we were in Campus Crusade for Christ, we spent a couple months a year at our training headquarters near San

Bernardino. A group of like-minded Campus Crusade leaders in search of historic Christianity began to meet there for breakfast in a supermarket restaurant that always opened early. At five o'clock in the morning, we'd gather five or six days a week to search the Scriptures.

Later, we realized that our journey to the Orthodox Christian Church actually began there in that restaurant as we studied and learned about God's design for the Church. Father Peter was always in attendance, contributing his foundational wisdom and perspective. I hardly even knew how to spell "Orthodox" in those days and yet, one step at a time, we began to believe that we had found our spiritual home.

Eventually, Fr. Peter and I left the staff of Campus Crusade for Christ, not because we were dissatisfied, but because we had one objective in mind. We were going to find Christ's Church. Whatever it was, we were going to find it and then submit to it.

In 1973, Fr. Peter and I attended a meeting in Dallas, Texas, with about two hundred former Campus Crusade staff members. Many of them were confused by our small band of brothers; why, they asked us, were we so intent on studying historic Christianity that we would leave behind our positions of leadership within our dynamic, respected Protestant organization?

After our group left Dallas, we flew to Memphis, Tennessee, and drove to the Gillquist home in Grand Junction so that we could spend several days clarifying our purpose and mission. In Grand Junction, seven of us made the commitment that we were going to stick together forever, until we found the Church of the New Testament, Christ's Body. We set out on our journey as Abraham did, to an unknown land, not really knowing where we were going (Heb. 11:8). Eventually and unexpectedly, we arrived on the doorstep of the ancient Eastern Orthodox Christian Church.

What were Fr. Peter's reasons for his unflagging quest for the truth? First, as a college student, he had made an irrevocable resolution to follow Christ, and he never wavered or flagged for a moment on that commitment. And secondly, Fr. Peter was committed heart and soul to the Church as the manifestation of the kingdom of God, whatever the cost of membership. That's what drove him.

After he became a priest and director for the Antiochian Department of Missions and Evangelism, it's what made him stand in the back of an airplane from New York, or Boston, or Chicago, on his way home to California. Over the years he developed back trouble and experienced terrible pain when seated. Scores of times he stood at the back of a plane except when the flight attendants made him sit down. Many people have no idea how much Fr. Peter's back hurt. He *couldn't* sit, and so he would stand for three or four hours as the plane made its way across the continent.

On the road, Fr. Peter had one subject that he returned to over and over: he talked about his Lord Jesus Christ. It didn't make any difference where he was; in an airplane, on an elevator, or eating at a restaurant, Fr. Peter would talk about Christ, and he would talk about the Church.

Some people didn't appreciate Fr. Peter. That made no difference to him. If you didn't like him, he liked you anyway. He was *for* you. His glass was never half-empty; rather, it was always at least three-quarters full. He was the most optimistic human being I have ever worked with, almost to a fault. In the thousands of hours we spent together, I never saw him in any frame of mind other than one of complete optimism. In the face of obstacles and difficulties, he always thought things were going to work out perfectly fine.

Father Peter was a man of impeccable integrity. I never saw him give the slightest ground to anything but utter honesty and truth. He wasn't one to exaggerate anything, either; he described things in a straightforward way, just as he saw them.

Whether he was writing or speaking, Fr. Peter was a master communicator. His book *Becoming Orthodox* became a bestseller, translated into numerous languages and read by spiritual seekers around the world. As well, it was entertaining to listen to him speak, because he always communicated with stories. Some of those stories are in this book.

In fact, Fr. Peter had said for years that *this* was the other book that he wanted to write. "I'd like to start from my youngest memories about how the Lord has been merciful to me and now to us," he said to an interviewer, "through those years of searching for the Church, learning how to be Orthodox, doing the missions and evangelism work; up through the years of retirement, where I continue experiencing His mercy . . . to share with other people the faithfulness of God in a way that I hope will motivate them to trust in Him more than they do now."

Father Peter was well educated, but he never presented ideas in an academic manner. He spoke directly to people, simply, without referring to obtuse or irrelevant concepts. When he finished speaking, he left his audience more motivated and spiritually warmed than they were when he started out. He helped us want to follow Christ.

A man of never-failing loyalty, Fr. Peter was utterly devoted to his family. Eventually, we became family when his oldest daughter and my fourth son were married. We share three grandchildren and two great-grandchildren. But family or no, he loved and was loyal to everyone he met. His loyalty to his own bishop, Metropolitan Philip of blessed memory, never wavered. His faithfulness and his loyalty to all Orthodox hierarchs were noteworthy, and he never spoke against any of them, even when others were doing so. Father was loyal to his friends and, yes, even to his enemies. Those who knew Fr. Peter knew that it never crossed his mind to betray anyone, friend or foe.

Father Peter loved his friends, and he was my dear friend. We could occasionally argue, but we never left an argument unfinished or unresolved; we always strove toward total agreement. He never demanded his own way, because love doesn't demand its own way. Our commitment to end all disagreements with agreement was part of the dynamic that made it possible for our group, the Evangelical Orthodox Church, to become a part of the canonical Orthodox Church.

Fr. Peter often preached the sermon "Crossing the Finish Line"; it is included in this book. I'll never forget that homily and how he challenged me to cross the finish line without faltering. Now Fr. Peter has crossed that line, triumphantly. He continues to be remembered by thousands of Orthodox Christians in America as a father in Christ, and many of his Protestant brethren hold him in high regard as well. Father Peter modeled for each and every one of us—regardless of our circumstances, backgrounds, or vocations—what it means to be a faithful, Christian man. If we follow in his footsteps, we will also live our lives to the glory of God.

CHAPTER 1

Earliest Memories

"Land of ten thousand lakes"

My parents told me they were married seven years before I was born on July 13, 1938, in Minneapolis, Minnesota. Dad was a clerk in his uncle's grocery store; my mother, Louise, enjoyed a career prior to marriage and then eventually settled into life as a stay-at-home mom, as many women did in the middle of the last century.

In one of my earliest memories, I am four years old and playing in the sandbox in the backyard of our rented home on 17th Avenue South in Minneapolis. I have a faint recollection of thinking about what I wanted to do when I grew up, and even then, the thought of serving God through Christian ministry flitted across my mind. This made enough of an impression on me that I remember the moment to this day. That was the first time I began to consider the option of making the ministry my lifetime profession.

A very influential man in my earliest years was our Lutheran pastor, Rev. Al Larson. At that time he was still a single man, and to this day I remember his piety; he definitely loved Jesus Christ,

Parker & Louise Gillquist

and he loved me. He would affectionately call me "my little man," and throughout my youth, as I moved through high school and then college, he would assure me that he was praying for me. What an impression that made on me!

We were a tight-knit family, since I was an only child. When I was in kindergarten, we bought our first house as a family; as a kid, I thought it was incredibly expensive at six thousand dollars. It was a 1920s Craftsman-style house in a nice south Minneapolis neighborhood, half a block from the grocery store where my father worked. I have memories of Dad walking to work rather than driving. In the dead of a Minnesota winter, he walked to work in his shirtsleeves without wearing a jacket. He loved the outdoors. Many of those mornings he walked to work in temperatures below zero.

Some of my favorite memories as a child are of the evenings when Dad would build a fire in the fireplace and the three of us would sit together. Occasionally Dad or Mom would read the Bible or a children's book. We snacked on popcorn and roasted marshmallows, and I basked in the security of our home.

I was blessed with some wonderful grandparents, aunts, and uncles. My paternal grandparents were both devout Christians.

Sadly, after my grandfather's first wife had given birth to their four children (of which my father was the eldest), she died from tuberculosis. Grandpa ended up marrying the nurse who had looked after her in her final months. Our grandma, "Nan," was a deeply committed Christian. Later, when I pieced the facts together, I concluded that it was most likely she who brought my grandfather to a deep and personal faith in Christ. They would always assure me they were praying for me.

One of my favorite memories of my grandparents is from a later period, when Marilyn and I were in college. By now we had become committed Christians. It was a warm night, perhaps during the late spring of Marilyn's freshman (and my junior) year at the University of Minnesota. Spontaneously we said, "Let's go over and see Grandma and Grandpa." They lived on a fairly busy street, so we had to park about four or five houses away. In the spring and summer in Minneapolis, it doesn't get dark until nine or ten at night, but as we walked toward their house, they were oblivious to our presence. There they sat on the porch swing in front of their lovely old Victorian home, holding hands. They were seventy-two years old at the time, and Marilyn and I looked at each other and said, "That's what we want to do when we're seventy-two!" They set a marvelous example for us, modeling for us that marriage is for a lifetime.

My maternal grandparents were not churchgoers, but they treated me like a prince. My grandfather was a very creative musician who taught me to play the guitar and introduced me to the mandolin. I remember watching him perform in one of the last minstrel shows in Minneapolis as the oldest person in the show.

Grandpa worked in the dry goods department of a local

department store in Minneapolis and made minimal wages. Grandma was a great cook, but they lived simply. I remember one time a letter arrived at their home, and Grandma was thrilled as she opened the envelope and discovered it was a check for one thousand dollars that she had received as an inheritance. She felt like she was the richest lady on the planet! Of course, back then, one thousand dollars was an enormous sum.

I had two favorite aunts. Aunt Raz was my maternal grandmother's sister and a deeply religious Roman Catholic. Often she would ride the streetcar up Nicollette Avenue in Minneapolis to come visit us. Located just off the streetcar stop on 48th Street was a pharmacy that sold incredibly good ice cream, and she'd always buy a pint of vanilla for us. Our house was just a half-block from the pharmacy, so the vanilla ice cream would still be nice and cold by the time she arrived at the front door. Aunt Raz modeled the spirit of giving to me—she always put other people ahead of herself.

My other favorite aunt was my mother's sister, Aunt Dell; I think I was her favorite nephew, too. Though she wasn't ostensibly a Christian woman, she exhibited incredible love for those around her and was a force for stability in the family.

When I was seven years old, my mother contracted tuberculosis. Back in those days, all they could do was put you in a sanatorium and wait for you to die. Of course, I was banned from seeing her for health reasons. After she had been in the sanatorium for ten months or so, I was allowed one visit. That's my last memory of Mom, because a few months after that, she died.

I was eight years old, and for the first time in my young life, I was experiencing the devastation that is wrought when parents lose their child and a child loses a parent. My mother's parents were inconsolable as they grieved the loss of their youngest daughter. Dad held up amazingly well, perhaps in part because he had been preparing for this day over the course of the year. I, on the other hand, was unprepared for her to die; while I was aware that she was sick, no one had told me it was terminal.

A key figure for Dad and me at this time was Pastor Al Larson. I remember he sat between us at the funeral. He didn't perform the funeral but rather attended as our friend, and that was incredibly helpful. The day after we buried Mom, my dad and I were driving down the lovely Minnehaha Parkway, which borders the creek of the same name and leads to the famous Minnehaha Falls in Minneapolis. I looked over at him and saw tears in his eyes. I was at a loss as to what I should say or do. It was the only time I ever saw Dad cry.

It was just the two of us who returned to the house now at day's end. However, soon after Mom's death, my maternal grandparents, Edward and Louise Blitsch, moved in to care for me while Dad worked. Often on Saturdays Dad and I arose early and hit the tennis court together. My goal was always to beat Dad, and one Saturday I surprised myself by doing just that. During that period of time, Dad really poured his life into mine inasmuch as he was able, and we became even closer than we had been before.

When I was twelve years old, my father married a woman from the church choir, and our family dynamic changed. My grandparents moved out and my stepmom moved in. Since then, I have always had a heart for kids who've lost a parent and ended up living with a stepparent, because for me it was not an easy thing to go through. It's natural for a child who loses a parent to expect, when the remaining spouse remarries, that things will be exactly the same as they were before. And of course, they never are. What I expected was a clone of my mom, and clones don't exist. Later, I realized that my stepmother, Marion, did everything she could to build a relationship with me, but my standards and the reality of who she was were two very different things. Thus our family experienced some years of turmoil, though thankfully, by God's grace, all differences and misunderstandings were eventually healed.

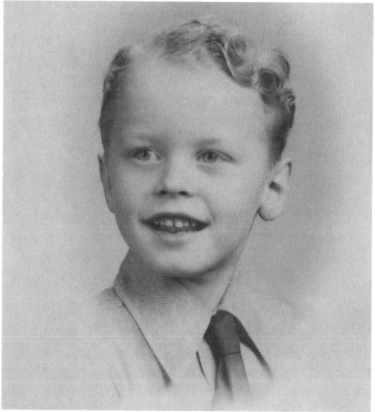

Young Peter

CHAPTER 2

The Race Set Before You

"If you agree to start, then I want you to cross this
finish line—no matter what."

In the ninth grade I contracted a disease called nephritis, a serious inflammation of the kidneys. At that time, about half the people with nephritis lived and the other half died. Fortunately I did not know that at the time. I was sick for much of my freshman year in high school and was tutored at home for much of my sophomore year.

When I was cured of this disease, I went back to school full time as a junior. By this time I was 6'4" and weighed about 135 pounds. I was so thin I had to run around in the shower in order to get wet. I noticed very quickly that all the guys who were popular were football players, and so I thought, "I really want to play football!" However, there was simply no way to follow through on this plan, given my limitations. After two weeks of practice in which guys who were 5'8" and 190 pounds came through the line to kill me (I was a split end), I decided I had to find another way to earn an athletic letter.

The only other fall sport at our school was cross-country.

Long-distance running has to be the hardest path toward earning a letter in a sport ever invented, but there was no other alternative. I remember the day I checked out the equipment and got on the bus to go to my first workout as a cross-country runner.

On that first day of practice, the bus deposited us at the start of a course that ran up and down several hills over a four-mile span. For those of us who were not in good shape or who had never run distance races before, our prospects on that late afternoon were particularly dismal.

Before he fired the starting gun, the coach said something to us that I have never forgotten. "What I am asking you to do today is to finish the race. If you don't plan to finish, then I do not want you to start. Simply stay where you are when the gun is fired. But if you start, then you will finish." He told us it was likely our legs would tighten and our stomachs would cramp. If so, we could slow down or even stop for a bit, but we could not quit once we had begun. "We'll wait here all night if need be," he told us. "If you agree to start, then I want you to cross this finish line—no matter what."

The first mile was almost euphoric. The brisk autumn air was a natural boost to my dogged determination to run a good race. But after a mile and a half or so, the joy began to fade. By two miles, whatever pleasure there had been in all of this effort was totally gone. From there on out, running became sheer drudgery. Some of my teammates were depositing the egg-salad sandwiches they had eaten for lunch at the school cafeteria into the tall grass and bushes at the edge of the course. Runners would stop for a bit, find some relief, and then fall back into the panting procession.

My legs started to cramp. I did not know thigh muscles could ever be so tired! I felt that my breath would leave me forever; my lungs and chest cavity were in almost unbearable pain as I approached the enormous hill near the two-and-one-half-mile mark. There was one thing and one thing only that kept me going: before I started, I had agreed to finish the race. My body said, *Quit!* My mind silently screamed, *Insanity!* But the choice had been made way back at the starting line when the gun went off. That issue was not open for renegotiation. There were no

Peter at his confirmation

options, no shortcuts. In inexpressible agony, I kept on running.

I can barely remember crossing the finish line. They said I came in fifth or sixth. But even that was not of first importance. Every ounce of energy I possessed had gone into simply reaching the goal. I could not believe I had made it.

We must have waited around twenty or thirty minutes for the rest of the team to finish. It was dark and bitterly cold by the time the last man crossed the line. We caught our collective breath, grumbled a bit to each other, and boarded the bus for home.

Over the years I have often thought back to that experience. It has served as an incredible picture of what it is to live the Christian life. The Scriptures repeatedly use the metaphor: our life with Christ is like running a race. It's not a sprint, mind you; it's a marathon!

Every race has three basic and essential components: the start, the race itself, and the finish. You need all three to win. You can have the fastest exit from the starting blocks known to man, but if you are slow on the turn or sloppy in the stretch, your record start will not be sufficient for victory. Or you can be unbeatable on the open track, but if you drop out fifty yards short of the goal, the rest of the effort is for naught. In any race, it's the first runner across the line who wins.

There will be varying degrees of speed and ability, of course. But when we are set apart to the Lord, His word to us is "Finish!"

Starting Blocks

Later, I often reflected on that early experience and compared it to the spiritual life. For the Christian, the obvious start of our faith is the New Birth. We come to Christ by faith. We have to remember that while saving faith is the all-important beginning of our life in Christ, we do not stop there. Paul writes, "Therefore, having been justified by faith, we have peace with God through our Lord Jesus Christ, through whom also we have access by faith into this grace in which we stand, and rejoice in hope of the glory of God" (Rom. 5:1–2).

I am troubled when we only emphasize the need to make a one-time "decision for Christ." Don't get me wrong: when I speak, I constantly call people to make decisions to follow Christ. But so often the implication is that if you simply say yes once, that decision will see you through. Let us be very clear on this: you cannot even qualify for the Christian race unless you place your faith in Christ. But the goal is not reached by a one-time response to Christ. The race requires perseverance down to the wire: "For we have become partakers of Christ if we hold the beginning of our confidence steadfast to the end" (Heb. 3:14). If crossing the line is not our goal, we are only cluttering up the track.

There is nothing cuter than a six-month-old baby. At this stage an infant develops eye contact, begins cooing, and generally learns to sleep all night. But if that is all the maturity someone shows at age fifteen, it is no longer cute. It is tragic. Let us have all the legitimate new births we can get. But let us be sure they are born into our household, the Church of God, where growth can occur and where they are given support to complete the race before them.

The Long Stretch

We obtain salvation by the grace of God in order to enter the race. It is by the power of the Holy Spirit that we run the course set before us. How crucial it is for us as we are running to keep our eyes fastened on "the prize of the upward call of God in Christ Jesus" (Phil. 3:14). It is here we must resist the temptation to think that just because we have made a good start, victory is automatic and quitting is impossible. The warning Paul issued to the first-century Galatians applies to us moderns as well: "You ran well. Who hindered you from obeying the truth?" (Gal. 5:7).

In 1 Corinthians 9:24–27, the apostle again uses a race to picture the Christian life. What a challenge he issues when he writes,

> *Do you not know that those who run in a race all run,*
> *but one receives the prize? Run in such a way that*
> *you may obtain* it. *And everyone who competes* for
> the prize *is temperate in all things. Now they* do it *to*
> *obtain a perishable crown, but we* for *an imperishable*
> crown. *Therefore I run thus: not with uncertainty. Thus*
> *I fight: not as* one who *beats the air. But I discipline*
> *my body and bring* it *into subjection, lest, when I have*
> *preached to others, I myself should become disqualified.*

Note that everyone runs to win. All do not tie for first place, but all run with winning in mind. Paul is not saying that only the one who finishes in first place will make it to heaven, but he intimates that it is an eternal mistake for any of us to assess our own abilities and then aim to finish second, or third, or fourth. It is plainly not our place to say, "Well, I have only a few talents" or "The Lord made me a thirty-fold Christian." We do not second-guess our spiritual equipping and run accordingly. Rather, we run to win.

Mark well that Paul's exhortation to the Corinthians includes a personal concern as well. To me, this is one of the most sobering passages in Scripture, for in his own steadfast aim to run well in the long stretch of his earthly Christian pilgrimage, Paul does not discount the possibility that "when I have preached to others, I myself should become disqualified" (1 Cor. 9:27). If the same one who writes, "For I am persuaded that neither death nor life, nor angels nor principalities nor powers, nor things present nor things to come, nor height nor depth, nor any other created thing, shall be able to separate us from the love of God which is in Christ Jesus our Lord" (Rom. 8:38–39) issues this incredible warning to himself, we need to listen all the more carefully.

Certainly, the Lord has spoken clearly, "I will never leave you nor forsake you" (Heb. 13:5). But we also must heed the passages of God's explicit warnings against apostasy, and they are there. We must hear and believe both the promise of glory and the warning of judgment. The fact is, if I quit the race, I will be disqualified. I cannot get around that truth in Scripture.

God exhorts us to get on with this business of living as holy people, staying on track and finishing the race set before us. If Paul was not enamored with his past service and did not take for granted his faithfulness to the Lord, then by all means neither should we.

Crossing the Line

If our starting point in Christ is the New Birth, if the race itself is to walk in the Spirit, the finish line is the "crown of life" (James 1:12). Is this victory attainable? Of course it is. Do not forget that it is through faith that you have come into living union with the One who is author and perfecter (finisher) of the race. Our Lord Jesus Christ not only conceived of and designed the course we run, but in His humanity He completed it, and He gives us His strength to do the same. We take part in His mission. When He prayed, "I have glorified You on the earth. I have finished the work which You have given Me to do" (John 17:4), He stood before His Father as victor in the battle. It is in His victory that we enter the competition ourselves. The One from whom we draw our life is already in the winner's circle.

Be it in athletics or in the Christian journey, we must finish the race in order to qualify for the victory circle.

CHAPTER 3

Sports and Music

*"There's a time a for joy
A time for tears
A time we'll treasure through the years
We'll remember always
Graduation day!"*

During the spring of my junior year in a new sports season, my dad told me that as a high school student he had tried his luck at high jumping and had been successful. I thought, "Well, if the gene pool is still intact, maybe this is something I can do." Having only high-jumped in gym a few times in my freshman year, I decided I'd try my luck on the track team.

The first meet of the year was a citywide event held at the indoor track at the University of Minnesota across town. In order to get into the meet, you had to qualify in the number one, two, or three slot from your own high school. I barely squeaked in as the third kid from Washburn High to be enrolled in the high-jump event.

In preparation, the runners, jumpers, and pole-vaulters would all practice on the indoor track three or four times to become accustomed to the facilities. There was a kid named Ron from West High School who had moved to Minneapolis from California, and the word had gotten out that back in California he had high-jumped six feet, an almost unheard-of feat for high school athletes at that time. I was barely clearing 5'3" and 5'4"! One day in practice I said to Ron, "Would you be willing to help me? I don't know what I'm doing." He proceeded to teach me some of the basics of the high-jump event, and I began to clear the 5'5" jumps.

The day of the meet came, and they started us jumping at 5'3"; half the guys dropped out by 5'4". There were eleven high schools in Minneapolis, and thirty-three guys were competing in the high jump. The bar was moved up to 5'6", a height I'd never cleared in my life, but I was able to sail over thanks to an incredible shot of adrenaline. At 5'7", Ron and I were the only two guys left in the event. I cleared 5'7", and Ron missed. Out of nowhere, I was the Minneapolis high school high-jump champion! I was absolutely flabbergasted.

The next morning when we read our newspaper, we found that I'd made the sports page of the *Minneapolis Tribune*. The football players and the cheerleaders said hi to me in the hall on the way to class, and my friends simply could not believe that, having never seriously high-jumped a day in my life, I was suddenly the best in the city. Of course, it made an incredible difference in my life. I believe it was the mercy of God, enabling me to have a sense of confidence I'd never had before.

In the realm of music, I experienced another significant high school milestone. I sang in the men's chorus as the lowest of the basses, and therefore I was chosen for a very sought-after solo on the song "Asleep in the Deep." The bass solo at the end of the song says, "Be-ee-ee-ee-ware!" and "-ware" was on a low D. There were two of us in the male chorus who could hit the note. I felt the other bass was actually better than I was, but the director chose me to be the soloist.

All my life I tended to freeze in front of a crowd, but to my surprise I discovered that while singing, I was at ease. Three other guys got together and formed a quartet, and I was asked to join them as the bass. At the end of my junior year and throughout my senior year, we sang at high school auditoriums and high school dances in the gym. Eventually, we actually got to be pretty good and were often featured at school events.

We learned popular songs from groups like the Four Freshmen. For our farewell program we learned a song called "I'll Be Seeing You," a very simple and poignant tribute to love and friendship that is still one of my favorites. We also learned a song called "Graduation Day" that was done by a Canadian group called the Rover Boys. Right after we learned it, the Four Freshmen arrangement of "Graduation Day" came out, which was way better, but by now we had learned this other arrangement and simply went with it.

At our graduation program we sang these two songs, and all the girls cried. It was an incredible evening, and again an aspect of my life that instilled confidence in me that I'd never felt I had.

The psalmist says, "The Lord formed me in my mother's womb" (Ps. 139:13, paraphrased), and even though those high school years were not years when I sought to follow God, nonetheless His promise was true: "I will never leave you nor forsake you." My parents loved God, brought me to church to be baptized into Christ as an infant, and made sure that on Sunday mornings I was in liturgy. Of my own free will, I had departed from the Christian life, but the Lord never departed from me. Only later was I to realize what an incredible consolation that was.

Peter, age 11, singing "White Christmas"

CHAPTER 4

Finding Marilyn, Finding Christ

*"I want a girl just like the girl
that married dear old Dad."*

One summer day in my mid-teens, at about nine in the evening, I was sitting on the front steps that led up to our house. I was thinking about life and what I wanted out of it. I still very deeply missed my mother. Later I couldn't say for sure where this resolve came from, but that night I made a vow that if I had nothing else in life, I would have a good marriage and a good home life. Somehow, even then, I knew this was more important than a successful career; it was more important than prominence; it was more important than financial security.

That night was a turning point in my life. From that point on, at an age when most other guys were out having fun and on the prowl, I was looking for that one girl with whom I would spend my life.

An old-time song popular in my grandparents' crowd at that time was "I Want a Girl." The words went:

I want a girl
Just like the girl
That married dear old Dad.
She was a pearl
And the only girl
That Daddy ever had.

That girl was my mom, and I dreamed of having a girl just like her as my wife.

The summer that followed my sophomore year of high school, I noticed that the girl down the street, Carolyn, ran with a really pretty bunch of girlfriends, so I concocted a scheme. I said to her, "What if every Friday night, we have a party at your house, and I'll furnish the records!" I was referring, of course, to phonograph records; back then we listened to 78s, with little holes in the center. "You furnish the Coke and the chips and dip, and I'll line you up with one of my friends, and you line me up with one of your friends, and we'll keep doing this until we both meet somebody we really like."

Bruce, a kid who lived across the street from Carolyn, had nursed an on-again, off-again crush on her for years. Every Friday night, Carolyn found a new girl for me to meet, and every Friday night I brought Bruce over. The first Friday night, Carolyn's beautiful cousin from Duluth was in town, but while we struck up a friendship, there was no chemistry. The second week I don't even remember who Carolyn lined me up with, but again, nothing clicked.

The third Friday night, Bruce and I arrived at Carolyn's house early because her dad had just gotten the first television set in the neighborhood. It was a round-screen set that looked like an old-fashioned Bendix automatic washer, and the picture was black and white with a ton of "snow," but that didn't matter. We were sitting on the couch watching one of the early TV variety shows, perhaps a comedian like Sid Caesar or Jack Benny.

The doorbell rang, and in walked this gorgeous, blonde-haired girl with a ponytail and the most beautiful eyes I'd ever seen. I said to myself, "That's the girl." And she was.

I don't tell this story because I think it's normal or because I think others should try to emulate my experience, but that's the way it happened to me.

As we had done the two previous Friday nights, we all went downstairs to Carolyn's unfinished basement, put some records on, danced, and enjoyed refreshments. Carolyn's dad took Marilyn home at ten o'clock because, after all, she was only fourteen and in the ninth grade.

The next week I called her up and walked the mile and a half from my house to her house, and we just went for a walk, circling several blocks near her home. Her neighborhood was a cut above ours. Ours was middle- to low-middle-class; hers was middle- to high-middle-class, and her father owned his own company. Nonetheless, her parents were warm and friendly, and I respected them right from the start.

Pretty soon school started. Our varsity football field separated my high school campus from her junior high school one, so almost every day after class I'd run over to Marilyn's locker at Ramsey Junior High and meet her there. We'd see each other for a few minutes, and then she'd head home and I'd head back to school for athletics or some after-school activity. We went together throughout my junior year and then my senior year. Of course, my eleventh-grade friends referred to Marilyn as "your ninth-grader." But I simply didn't care. I knew she was the girl.

After I graduated from high school and went off across town to the University of Minnesota as a freshman, I knew I had to immerse myself in my studies or I wouldn't succeed, since I wasn't a natural student. By now Marilyn was in her junior year of high school, and she had become incredibly popular in her class; eventually, she was class secretary and president of every organization she joined.

On New Year's Eve of my freshman year of college, we went out on a date and got into a ferocious argument. Ironically, neither of us could remember later what it was about. It had to be the worst night of my life. I dropped her off at her house and heard her say the words, "I never want to see you again."

The next day, New Year's Day, I went over to her house and found her dad out shoveling snow. He said, "I suppose you want to see Marilyn," and I said, "Yes."

He said, "She doesn't want to see you."

I said, "I've come over to apologize."

He said, "I'm really sorry. I've been married twenty-five years, and I still don't understand women. She doesn't want to see you." So that began a period of more than a year of separation, and it was the toughest year of my life.

My sophomore year of college, I joined the Sigma Alpha Epsilon (SAE) fraternity on campus and immersed myself in the social life a fraternity house affords. We were by no means "Animal House," but nonetheless it was certainly not a spiritual hothouse of any kind. One of our songs said:

It was not for knowledge
That we came to college,
But to raise hell while we're here.

The first time I heard those lyrics, I thought back to my mom and the standards she had set for me, and I thought to myself, "I'll never raise really bad hell, but I want to have some fun."

In the year I was separated from Marilyn, I went through what a lot of guys go through who are in the same boat. I tried to fall in love again, and it simply didn't work. The social life, the parties, the football weekends—these all became perfunctory. You had a date, you treated her well, you did what was on the schedule, but deep down, you knew you weren't really enjoying life.

A popular song at that time said:

Laughing on the outside,
Crying on the inside,
Because I'm still in love with you.

When that song came on the radio, I couldn't stay dry-eyed, because it summed up exactly the way I felt. Fortunately, in my sophomore year I had a roommate in the fraternity who had been an all-state high school football player. I was 6'4" and probably weighed 140 to 150 pounds; he was 6'5" and weighed about 210. To be honest, I was scared to death of him. He had gotten injured and no longer played football, but to me he still was the kind of guy I would not want to cross.

One night we were in the room studying, each of us at his own desk, and Kirk said, "Who are you going to take to the spring formal?"

I said, "I have no idea."

He said, "You must have somebody in mind."

I said, "Well, back in high school, I went out with this incredible girl that I still love, but we had a falling-out and I've not seen her or talked with her since."

He said, "Why don't you call her?"

I said, with a muffled voice, "I don't think she'd want to go out with me."

He said, "Well, why don't you just call her and see?"

I whined back, "I don't think so."

He finally slapped his hand on his desk and said, "Call her!" and I knew he meant it. The phone booth in the fraternity was right across the hall from our room. I stepped out of my dorm room and, of course, I still remembered her number by heart. I called her, and she answered.

I said, "This is Peter."

"Oh! How are you?"

"I'm fine. How are you doing?"

She said, "I'm fine; I'm doing well."

"This is a shot in the dark, but next month we're having our spring formal for our fraternity at a country club, and I wondered if you'd like to go with me."

She said, "I really would," and I about fainted.

I couldn't wait until the night of the formal arrived. It was a beautiful dinner party. All the guys rented tuxes; all the girls wore party gowns. It was a sit-down dinner followed by a dance with a live band that played all the great old romantic standards of the 1940s and 1950s (the year was 1955). Four of us guys in the fraternity who had formed a quartet sang some songs during the

Peter and Marilyn at his ROTC formal in 1959

dance, and Marilyn—a state championship piano player—was our accompanist. By the time Marilyn and I finished the first dance, I knew we were back together for keeps.

We began to see each other regularly on the campus where she was now a freshman and I was a junior. One night I asked her why it was she said "yes" when I called her to ask her to go to the formal. She said, "I'd like to tell you it was because I missed you, but the real reason was that the guy I was going out with had stood me up the weekend before you called. I was looking for payback time!"

Later, when we became Christians, we realized that "all things work together for good to those who love God, to those who are the called according to *His* purpose" (Rom. 8:28), and that none of us do anything out of one hundred percent pure motives. We smile and thank God that in the midst of all we both went through in that time we were apart, God found a way to bring us back together.

In the spring of my junior year, probably around April—by then we had been back together for about a year—the phone rang in the chapter house, and somebody said, "Gillquist, it's for you!" This was back in the days when girls rarely called guys, and this was Marilyn, so I knew it had to be important. By this time we were pinned, which means (in fraternity and sorority parlance) engaged-to-be-engaged.

I picked up the phone, and she said, "Honey, the most wonderful thing just happened to me today."

I thought, *Does she have a rich aunt who died and left her a bundle of money?* I asked, "Okay, well, what is it?"

She said, "This morning I gave my life to Jesus Christ."

"What are you talking about? You've gone to church all your life. You even thought at one time you'd be a missionary. What on earth do you mean?"

She said, "Well, I don't know about you, but ever since I've been in college, the Lord has not been real to me, and this morning, through the help of a friend, we prayed together, and I really gave my life over to Him. I just want you to know that I want to be a Christian and put Him first for the rest of my life."

I got so frustrated I hung up on her.

About a week later, I called her back and apologized, and by then she was more committed than ever. On her drive to school she'd been listening to KTIS, the local Christian radio station. She was studying her Bible and praying.

I began to think, *Who wants to marry a religious girl?* I would take Marilyn out for a movie or for supper, and she'd get into my car and immediately put on the Christian radio station. It just drove me nuts! I said, "I'm willing to talk with you about this, but don't push me."

There was an older widow in town named Grandma Mac whom I had never met. Grandma Mac was about seventy-five years old and was an old-fashioned Presbyterian who had received a fresh dose of the Holy Spirit somewhere along the way. She was, in the vernacular of the Evangelical Christians of the 1950s, a "prayer warrior." This meant she spent three or four hours a day in prayer. Many of the pastors in town and other Christian workers would talk with her and ask her to put people on her prayer list. Marilyn was introduced to Grandma Mac through the campus friend who'd brought her to her renewed faith in Christ. It turns out, I was not only on Grandma Mac's prayer list, I was Number One on her prayer list!

If you were on the prayer list, it was over for you, and I suppose if you were Number One on the prayer list, you didn't have a chance in the world. Through her prayers and God's grace, I found myself growing tender toward the Gospel in a way that I sensed was almost out of my hands.

A week or so later, young men from a Christian group called Campus Crusade for Christ spoke in our fraternity house. A couple of people shared their spiritual stories, and then a main speaker talked about Christ. A young man who was captain of our football team at Minnesota that year shared his story; he was quite well respected, and I listened closely.

Yet he wasn't the one who made the greatest impression on me. Instead, I was most moved by the words of an international student named Victor, who had come to America to study for his undergraduate and now doctoral degrees. He had come to the United States as a Hindu. He told us he came for two reasons: (1) to get a great education and (2) to investigate Christianity. He had looked into all the living religions of the world, and in so doing, discovered that the founder of just one of them had claimed to be God—Jesus Christ. Victor told us, "Mohammed said he was a prophet, Buddha said he was enlightened, and Jesus said, 'I am the light of the world. I and My Father are one. He who has seen Me has seen the Father.'"

That night, I realized in a new way that the Lord Jesus Christ was absolutely unique in all of history. He was the Son of God who had become man, for us and for our salvation, without ever ceasing to be God.

The emcee that night asked if any of the guys were interested in starting a Bible study. He offered to come over to the house one evening a week to teach us. I thought to myself, "I'm going to give this one last shot," so I volunteered to try to get the interested guys together.

We chose the Book of Philippians because it's short, and we were only five or six weeks away from finals at the end of the spring quarter. One night in prayer before falling asleep, thanks to what I was learning in the Bible study, I simply committed my life to Christ and told Him I would do whatever He wanted me to do. I asked Him to forgive my sins and to make me a new person. The last sentence of the prayer was this: "From here on out, I'm Yours, and I'll do whatever You ask me to do."

The next morning, I called Marilyn and told her what I'd done; she was shocked. From that point forward, we began to relate to each other as Christians. We'd pray together on dates and did our best to live lives that were pleasing to the Lord. That summer we attended two Christian conferences together; they were very helpful to us. That fall, we both went back to campus, she to her sorority house and I to my fraternity house. Many collegians would seek us out to talk, even those who we never expected would be interested in Christianity.

By Christmas, I was convinced that what God had first spoken to me about, fifteen years before as I played in my sandbox, was going to become a reality. I wanted to do nothing else with my life but to serve Him.

Marilyn and I were married at the end of my senior year in the largest Lutheran church in the world at that time, Mount Olivet.

School was still in session, so all our friends attended, as well as all our high school friends and all our parents' friends. We ended up with a thousand people at our wedding!

Down the aisle! Wedding day—May 14, 1960

CHAPTER 5

Early Marriage, Education

"Seek ye first the kingdom of God."

I had managed to save five hundred dollars for our honeymoon and the start of our life together. Marilyn had visited the city of Chicago as a high school kid and had fallen in love with it. Her dad offered to fly us to Chicago; then we planned to take the train home, because it's such a pretty ride from Chicago back up north to Minneapolis.

And so it was that after the wedding, we flew down to Chicago on a Saturday night at about midnight. We were scheduled to take the train home Wednesday morning, which would put us at the train depot at three in the afternoon that day. This way we could return to campus, finish up the last couple weeks of classes, and then go into finals week.

(Marilyn's mom had a blood pressure problem and felt very poorly in hot weather, so she had given us a choice to get married either in May or the following November. Without hesitation we had said May, and that's why the wedding took place before I graduated from college.)

It was the Monday of our honeymoon in Chicago, and the

phone in our hotel room rang. I heard the voice of one of my fraternity brothers on the other end of the line. He had been an attendant at our wedding and was a friend I'd known and dearly loved since high school. He said, "I'm calling to see if you'd be willing to come home a day early from your honeymoon to compete in an intramural track meet. Here's the situation: if we win the track meet, we can win the All-Intramural trophy for the year, which will be a tremendous rushing asset for the fraternity. We've projected the various events; in order for us to win the track meet, Jim will do the 220 and the 440 and win, Bruce will do the 100-yard dash and win, and if you can come and win the high jump, we can win the track meet!"

I said, "Jim, do you have any idea what it is you're asking? This is my one and only honeymoon. As much as I love you guys, I've got to put my wife ahead of my friends."

He said, "I understand, but we really want you to come back and do this."

I said, "Here's what I'll do. Marilyn and I will pray today that the track meet will be rained out tomorrow. If it is, we'll be arriving Wednesday at three o'clock at the downtown train depot; you can meet us there, pick us up, and we'll go to the meet."

So we prayed about it, asking God to work a miracle and rain the meet out. We totally forgot about it from that point on—which is what anyone would do on a honeymoon—and boarded the train Wednesday morning to go back to Minneapolis.

When we hit the depot and got off, there were Jim and a couple of other friends, holding a pair of sweatpants, a pair of track shoes, and a jockstrap, saying, "The meet was rained out yesterday. It has already started this afternoon! We've registered you, and if we hurry, we can get you back to the meet before the bar goes up so high that you won't want to compete."

We got our luggage and rushed back to the university campus. Jim and the others dumped me at the entrance to the football stadium. Marilyn took a seat in the stands, and I went out onto the track. At that point, the bar was probably set at 5'5". I had not high-jumped in three years! I remember I slipped on the first try and fell into the pit, and then I got scared. I thought my high-jumping days were over.

On the second try, I again felt a huge rush of adrenaline similar to the one I'd experienced as a junior in high school, and I sailed over the bar as it edged up to 5'8", 5'10", 5'11", and 6'. At 6', there were two of us left. One was Bobby Bell, who was an incredible tight end at the University of Minnesota and later went on to play for the Kansas City Chiefs and become an NFL Hall-of-Fame member. He was competing for the "independents," that is, the dorm kids. I was competing for the fraternity championship, which was separate from the independent championship.

Both Bobby Bell and I cleared 6', and they put the bar up to 6'1", a height I had never attained. Bobby cleared the bar, and I was sure I couldn't. Lo and behold, I did! At the 6'2" height, we both missed, and we went out as co-champions. Bobby was awarded the independent trophy, and I got the fraternity trophy. Because I won the high jump, we won the meet, and because we won the meet, we won the intramural trophy.

That day, my friends and I learned in a very practical way that if you put Christ and the Kingdom first, everything else falls into place. It was another step at the beginning of my journey as a married man that underscored for me the priority of putting

Christ and the Church first, one's family second, and other priorities and endeavors third. It was a lesson I never forgot.

Of course, I endured endless kidding from the day of the track meet on to the end of the school year. What is it about a honeymoon, they wanted to know, that lets you jump higher than you've ever jumped in your life, having not practiced at all for three straight years? I still don't know the answer to that question.

After I graduated from the University of Minnesota in the spring of 1960, the only goal on the horizon as far as we were concerned was to find God's will and do it. We both had the palpable sense of His mercy upon us.

When I graduated from college, the call to the Christian ministry was as strong as ever. Having been brought up in the Lutheran Church, I simply assumed I'd be a Lutheran pastor. However, through the counsel of a friend, I had come to feel the Lutheran Church was moving in directions I could no longer support: questioning the inspiration of the Scriptures, the Resurrection, and the Virgin Birth of Christ. Even though this infection resided mostly in the seminaries and not yet in the parishes, I felt that as a new believer it would be unwise for me to subject myself to teaching that I knew in my heart was not true.

Some of my Campus Crusade friends had been very impressed with the ability of the teachers and preachers who were coming out of Dallas Theological Seminary, a nondenominational school in Texas. In the spring before our wedding, I applied to Dallas and was accepted. After our May wedding, Marilyn and I got in our beautiful old 1951 Buick Roadmaster and headed south.

When we first arrived on campus and were walking through

the mailroom, we met a couple destined to be our lifelong friends, Dave and Sande Sunde. David and Sande had gone to Western Michigan University, where he had played basketball. They were kindred spirits. I remember one night that first year, Marilyn and I were at home, missing our family. From out of the blue, I called Dave Sunde and said, "Why don't you and Sande come over for a slumber party?" They were crazy enough to do it, so we gave them our bed, and we slept in the little single bed in my office. We stayed up playing board games and had so much fun! We all still remember that night as one of the most memorable nights of our first year at seminary.

At Dallas, my favorite professor was Professor Howard Hendricks. He was an incredibly gifted communicator who taught homiletics and preaching, and he was a vocal advocate for strong and stable marriages. If I remember his story correctly, he was an orphan who had been adopted into a Christian home and nurtured spiritually by his adoptive parents. All he wanted to do was serve the Lord.

Toward the end of each class, he would say something personal to the guys, such as, "Men, when's the last time you took your wife's face into your hands and told her you loved her more than life itself?" or "Tonight, I want you to stop at a flower stand on the way home, and if you can afford one rose, buy it and bring it home to her." Then another time he said, "Learn to give your wife a gift for no reason at all. She expects something on her birthday or on your anniversary, but learn to give her a little gift just because you love her." Those are the things that stayed with me in my memory of Howard and Jeanne Hendricks. I later worked as their editor for Thomas Nelson Publishers.

One Saturday morning, we'd invited our Campus Crusade collegians and some of the seminary guys for breakfast at our apartment. On Friday afternoon after school, Marilyn and I went out to shop at the grocery store. We both looked at each other and realized she had no money in her purse, I had no money in my wallet—this was back before the days of credit cards, so charging wasn't an option—and there was nothing in the checking account.

As we walked through the front entryway of the apartment house by the mailboxes, I realized we'd never picked up the mail. We checked the mail and saw that we had received one letter that day, with no return address and no postmark on the envelope. For some reason, the stamp was canceled but there was no postmark. We opened the letter up and there was a ten-dollar bill, which in those days enabled us to buy bacon, sausage, eggs, and bread for toast.

Throughout our lives this kind of thing happened. That day, we hadn't even known we needed the money, and yet there it was, a total surprise! Over the years, these loving gestures of provision from our Lord have caused us to give thanks to Him; He has known our needs before we have even asked Him.

At the end of my first year at Dallas Seminary, Bill Bright, the president of Campus Crusade, telephoned me and asked if I'd be willing to move to Chicago, start a chapter of the college fellowship at Northwestern University, and form a board of men to underwrite the work there.

In college, I had been commissioned as a second lieutenant through the ROTC program and had signed my life away in my junior year. This meant I'd made a commitment to serve in active duty for two or three years. In those days, the active duty assignment could be deferred if one was studying in seminary, so I explained to Bill that I'd need to attend seminary somewhere in Chicago. He understood this and suggested I attend Wheaton Graduate School just outside the city. Wheaton was evangelist Billy Graham's alma mater and was highly regarded in Christian circles for its high educational and spiritual standards.

In addition to accepting me, the administration at Wheaton Graduate School graciously waived the ninety-hour requirement for an undergraduate student to graduate and allowed Marilyn to attend Wheaton for her senior year of college, where she majored in music. I enrolled in the graduate school and took a minimal load so I could devote myself to the Campus Crusade work.

Unlike the year at Dallas Seminary, which had been spiritually encouraging, that year at Wheaton was tougher. By 1962, the attitudes of the sixties were emerging. A lot of the Christian kids at the graduate school were asking questions I had already settled when I became a Christian in college. Many of the professors seemed to provide rational answers rather than spiritual ones. However, I encountered two spiritual giants in that Wheaton year who left their mark on me: the college president, V. Raymond Edman, and Chaplain Evan Welsh, a godly, warm, Christ-centered man who was an especial help to me personally.

By the next year, things had gotten going so well at Northwestern that we decided to move closer to campus. We found a small apartment in Evanston, Illinois, and through the help of the Campus Crusade board, we plunged ever more deeply into ministry to college students.

CHAPTER 6

First Fixer-Upper

*"I'd like to give you the two thousand dollars
you need to buy the house."*

After living in a two-bedroom apartment in Evanston near the campus of Northwestern University for a time, we realized we were in need of a house. With four children, things were getting crowded! We began checking the papers and at first found a house up in Wilmette. Thankfully, a good friend said, "You cannot afford this," and steered me clear of buying it, knowing we'd have been in over our heads.

A place came up on Main Street in an old residential section of Evanston, and the owner wanted $21,500 for the house. It was in a great neighborhood, but the house itself had been trashed. The previous renter had torn the wall out between the living room and dining rooms, exposing the wooden studs, the electric conduit, and the heat vent. Prospective buyers would tour the house, and the wife would say, "No way am I living in this mess!"

Upstairs, there were two bedrooms next to each other—you walked out of one, down the hall, and into the second one. The tenant had evidently decided that was too much effort and had knocked down part of the wall between bedrooms without doing the finishing work. It was just naked. I said to the home's owner, "The best I can do, if I line everything up, is $19,300, maybe $19,400. I know the house is worth more than that, but that is all I can offer you."

He said, "Well, I'll take it."

Now the question came: how would we finance it? I had been able to save about two thousand dollars for the down payment, but I needed another two thousand to meet the twenty-percent requirement. I'd developed this nasty habit over the years of asking wealthy people to "pray for our financial needs," and I determined with Marilyn that this time we were not going to do that. We wanted this house to either be God's will or not be God's will, and I didn't want to pad my chances by resorting to something I felt by now was just not right.

The last meeting I ever had with my Campus Crusade staff people included many of our staff from the Midwest, all of whom were essentially penniless. At that meeting, I explained to them that we were in the throes of trying to buy this home. I confessed to them that I now felt I shouldn't be asking rich people to pray—instead, I was asking them for their prayers that God would somehow open the door for us to be able to purchase the place.

I explained that I needed two thousand dollars, and I knew none of them were in any position to help out other than through prayer. Together, the group prayed that God would somehow bring this money in, if buying this house fulfilled His will. After the time in prayer, I walked outside.

One of our student staff members from Bradley University followed me out. "You've got the money," he said.

I said, "What are you talking about?"

"You had no way of knowing this, but a couple of years ago, my father died and left me a nice inheritance, and I'd like to give you the two thousand dollars you need to buy the house." Then he said, "If you can never pay it back, that's fine. If you can pay it back, it will make life much easier for my mom, who will know about this." Given the fact I had no idea that he had any money at all, I accepted with great thanksgiving!

Now the only step was to secure a loan. There was a Christian man named Mr. Anderson who was quite well known in Evangelical circles in and around Chicago. He was the president of several suburban banks, including the Bank of Evanston. I had never met him, though I had met his wife at a Christian women's luncheon where I had spoken. I called him up cold turkey and explained that I had my down payment lined up but needed a loan to finance the purchase of the home. He asked me, "What is your collateral?"

And I said, "Mr. Anderson, my collateral is my word. I've never defaulted on anything in my life, and I don't plan to start with you. But this is our first home, and I have no stash of possessions to back up the loan."

I don't know what his reason was, but through the grace of God he said, "I'll grant you the loan."

The day of closing came, and Marilyn and I got in the car to drive to the bank. I'd looked at our checkbook, and there was a dollar-something in the checking account, which you could get away with back in those days. I remember holding her hand and praying, "Lord, somehow, we need a hundred dollars today. There's no money to buy groceries. The cupboards are bare; the refrigerator's bare. So we ask that you would grant us, somehow, a hundred dollars, so that we can get going and feed the kids."

I remember going upstairs to the boardroom at the bank and attending the closing. When it was over, we shook hands with the former owner and his wife and the attorneys, and went back downstairs and out into the parking lot to drive to the new home, just a mile away. As we were exiting the parking lot, the former owner came running toward us with a big smile on his face and a white, business-sized envelope in his hand. I said to Marilyn, "There's the hundred dollars."

She rolled down the window, and he came up to the car and said, "The one thing I never got to do was clean the attic, and it's a mess. This'll more than cover what you need to have someone clean the attic out."

I said, "Bob, you're an answer to prayer." After he left, we opened the envelope, and there indeed was a check for one hundred dollars.

Through this whole event I learned better than I ever had how God is merciful to those who love Him, and how He answers the prayers of those who need His help, because to us, this was a total miracle.

We set about to restore this old Victorian treasure of a house to its original grandeur as much as was possible. Fortunately a friend had moved in with us and was willing to do the work in exchange for the free room and board that we were more than happy to offer. We spent that next year restoring the house, even trying to get some of the original colors of the 1880s for both the interior and exterior paint. I would tell my friends, "The next move I make will be out of here horizontally, feet first, with several men carrying me. I have no desire to ever live anywhere else."

During the year we lived in that old house in Evanston, I had begun writing a book entitled *Love Is Now*, which went on to become a Christian bestseller. In preparation for doing that work, I attended the Billy Graham Writers' Institute held each summer in Minneapolis. The institute's mentor was Dr. Sherwood Wirt, the editor of Graham's *Decision* magazine, a publication with a circulation of three million. For some reason, Dr. Wirt liked me. I was enthusiastic about being a Christian, I was enthusiastic about communicating the Gospel, and he was enthusiastic about mentoring young writers in need of help and direction.

At that writers' conference, we began a friendship that would last for decades. Although I'd gotten Bs and Cs in high school English, he was the one who convinced me that, if I worked at it, I could write. He also offered practical advice about writing that has proved helpful to me all of my adult life. Interestingly, Dr. Wirt had also known and admired a young, energetic youth

Summer of 1967 in Minneapolis, MN

leader named Jon Braun. Jon put in several years as an assistant pastor at Park Avenue Covenant Church in Minneapolis while also coaching the track team and serving as the chaplain at Minnehaha Academy, the city's prominent Evangelical high school. Sherwood Wirt had always admired Jon's ability to preach the Gospel and communicate with youth. Incredibly, Jon would later become Fr. Jon Braun, an Antiochian priest, my dear friend, and my daughter's father-in-law. It's a small world.

When it came time for Zondervan to publish my first book, Sherwood Wirt offered to write the foreword, which was a huge plus for me as a first-time author. He ended up being one of the "men of mercy" that God has repeatedly sent to me throughout my life.

A year after purchasing the Evanston fixer-upper, I was offered a job at the University of Memphis as Director of Development. Not for the first time, we realized that for Christians, nothing is permanent. We decided to sell our home in Evanston and move to Memphis. By this time, some of us on the Campus Crusade staff were pursuing the dream of finding the New Testament Church, and we had learned that there was a group of students on the campus who were doing the same. We believed that we could be part of and help form this core of people as we mutually sought to attain this elusive goal.

We put our lovingly remodeled house on the market, and it sold for a gross price of $36,000, just a year after we had bought it for $19,400. By the time we'd settled up with the real estate people and the bank and paid my friend Rick his two thousand dollars back, I had earned ten thousand dollars profit on an investment for the first time in my entire life. It had been totally unintended.

CHAPTER 7

Memphis: Home Church and Youth Ministry

"And he went out, not knowing where he was going." (Hebrews 11:8)

W hen we got to Memphis, we were tempted to buy a home for $29,000 and invest the profit from our Evanston house. Yet when we thought twice about it, we concluded we didn't need a home worth $29,000 when it was possible to buy a beautiful place in Memphis for just $19,000, which was exactly what we did. In our search for a home, we looked for a place that would hold a lot of people, since our plan was that we'd be hosting a house church. In the beautiful Central Gardens area of Memphis, we bought a 3300-square-foot place with a huge living room, dining room, entry hall, and stairway up to the second floor. The house could hold 125 people.

This began the next chapter in our life, the story of our three years in Memphis, working for the university and seeing the first efforts of a very primitive expression of the church take hold. Having moved into our new home in Memphis, we began to hold a house church on Sunday mornings with a group of about thirty people, most of whom were students at the university. We made a commitment that when a person would come to faith in Jesus Christ, we would baptize him or her, and we would serve communion every Sunday morning, as was the practice in the New Testament Church (Acts 20:7).

We decided together that our goal was not to grow numerically but to grow in our understanding of what the Church is all about as the Body of Christ. We sought to make worship the center of our efforts, above and beyond anything else. The Lord had taught that the first and greatest commandment is to love the Lord your God with all your heart, soul, mind, and strength, and secondly, to love your neighbor as yourself. By now we had come to understand that the way we express our love to God is in worshiping Him. One friend defined worship as "loving Him back."

At the same time, we had a sense that we didn't know what we were doing. Certainly communion was at the center of worship, but how the rest of the church service was supposed to look, we simply were not clear.

Much to our surprise, because the people who came on Sunday morning were so responsive to our worshiping together as a close-knit community, they began to invite their friends. One Sunday morning, a lady who lived on the next block and was a hairdresser for one of the women in the group came and placed her faith in Jesus Christ, right on the spot. She talked about how she'd been looking for God and was so thrilled to belong to a group of Christians. She was part of the counter-culture movement in Memphis, and she began inviting other people to join us on Sunday mornings.

The upshot of this was that we weren't sure who would be there on Sunday mornings, and often we had nearly as many non-Christians as Christians attending. We suspended the Sunday morning meeting because we felt we could not serve communion to just anybody who came. Instead, we held worship on Sunday nights and emphasized evangelism and outreach to the community rather than worship.

I can still remember one Sunday evening leading a group, first in singing and then in the study of the Scriptures. The thought crossed my mind, "I really don't know what I'm doing!" As I think back over my life, there were a lot of times when I felt that way. For instance, on my first day of high school, I was scared to death. I'd never been a high school student before. How would I relate to my peers? Then I went off to college and joined a fraternity, and again, I felt I was totally unaware of what I was doing. Falling in love and getting married was the same way: I'd never been a husband before. After that came the dramatic shock of having our first child, knowing I really didn't know how to be a father.

Here again in Memphis, I was facing the challenge of leading a group who wanted to become a New Testament expression of the Church, and yet I felt totally inadequate to the task. As the years have unfolded, one of my favorite passages has become Hebrews 11:8: "By faith Abraham obeyed when he was called to go out to the place which he would receive as an inheritance. And he went out, not knowing where he was going." This verse was such a comfort to a person like myself. I knew the goal of finding the New Testament Church was before me, and yet I had no idea how to get from the dream to the reality.

In addition to my work with the university, I was appointed to the Mayor's Drug Commission. This was the early seventies, and the drug scene was well established in the U.S. Henry Lobe, the mayor of Memphis, had heard of our Sunday evening gatherings and asked if I would be part of the commission that was trying to help the younger generation steer clear of the whole drug scene.

Because of my contact with the commission, I worked in conjunction with some of the judges in Memphis. One day I received a call from the secretary of one of the judges, a dear Christian, who said, "There's a girl who's in jail here for drug possession and drug use, and she has told us she would like to become a Christian and escape this way of life. Would you be willing to go see her?"

I had learned over the years that in situations like this I should never go alone, so I called a close friend who was part of our Sunday morning group and asked if he'd be willing to go to the county jail with me. As we talked with the girl about Christ, it became apparent to me that her real goal was not first and foremost to become a Christian but to get out of jail. I informed her that I had no power to grant that wish, but I would certainly be willing to work with her personally to come to a place where she would be willing to commit her life to Christ.

In the weeks ahead, she was released from jail and ended up moving back in with her boyfriend in an old, abandoned mansion that had been leased to a group of hippies for something like a hundred dollars a month. It turned out that the boyfriend was the one who was most interested in being a Christian, and we had the joy of bringing him to Christ and baptizing him over the course of that next year. Later we found out that not only had he been the number-one drug dealer in Memphis, but he had also been the leader of the Satan-worshipers in the city.

After his conversion, Marilyn and I were visiting with the hippies in the old mansion one evening. I asked our newly converted friend to tell me, just briefly, some of what Satan-worshipers do. He told us about the séance his group had conducted one night. "I don't know how to put this into words, but we believe the big kahuna himself appeared to us."

I asked, "What was that like?"

He replied, "Well, you know us Christians. We talk about the reality of being filled with the Holy Spirit. That night, we sensed we were filled with pure evil, and it was the eeriest thing I've ever experienced in my life."

What a joy it was to see this young man renounce his former life, embrace his commitment to Jesus Christ, and become part of the fledgling community that met at our home in Memphis.

I remember another event in Memphis in the spring of 1970. Young people from those years remember the tragedy at Kent State University; a large group of students had taken on the National Guard in a fight for control of the campus, and in the fracas that followed, six students were shot and killed on the campus property. This ignited the kids who were already part of the anti-Vietnam War peace movement.

At the University of Memphis, a group of radical students had traveled from the East Coast in an effort to organize a revolt on the campus against the administration and against "the establishment" of the city. They pressured the head of the university into hosting a memorial for the Kent State students on the mall of the campus, and the student body president was charged with putting together a program that would be a loosely defined memorial service. I was asked if I would be the final speaker.

A few days later, it was time for the event to begin. Those of us participating in the program stood on the steps of the administration building overlooking some five thousand students gathered on the mall. We had been told that immediately after the memorial program, the more radical elements in the activist groups planned to march to the ROTC building and burn it down, as they had done on other campuses.

This was one of the few times in my life I simply could not decide what God wanted me to say. A short time before the program began, I went into a stall in the men's room on the first floor of the administration building, just down the hall from my office, and fervently prayed that God would somehow give me the words. I had absolutely no sense of what He wanted me to express.

It came time for us to walk out to address the gathering, and I still had nothing in my heart to share. The first speaker was one of the denominational chaplains on campus, and he gave as awful a presentation as I've ever heard. I don't remember the second speaker, but the third speaker was the president of the Black Students' Association, and he gave a tremendously impassioned talk that was actually a hard act to follow. The student body president gave me what—especially for that time—would have been the worst introduction possible. "And now speaking for the administration, I present to you Peter Gillquist!"

On the way to the podium, the Holy Spirit said to me, "I want the first word out of your mouth to be 'Jesus.'" I stepped up to the mike, drew a breath, and said, "Jesus . . . said, 'I am the Resurrection and the Life. He that believes in Me, though he were dead, yet shall he live. Because I live, you shall live also.'" At that moment, I thought back to the promise of the Lord in Matthew

10:19, "But when they deliver you up, do not worry about how or what you should speak. For it will be given to you in that hour what you should speak." From that point on in my address, the words simply flowed as I talked about the fact that all of us are in need of a new beginning and a new life, and only Jesus Christ can offer that life and fulfill His promise to us.

In my speech, I segued from who Jesus Christ is into the hope of the coming Kingdom of God. I told the crowd how as a college student I had given my life to Jesus Christ, and how radically He had changed my life. I was now focused on Him instead of simply the things of this world. I closed my remarks with a challenge to each of those present to give their lives to Jesus Christ and to take the tragedy being commemorated and learn from it. Our identity must be with Christ in His Kingdom rather than with the fleeting kingdoms of this world.

I didn't comprehend at the time what an impact my remarks had made on this crowd of people. Instead of marching to the ROTC building as planned, the people simply dispersed and went their separate ways. In the days that followed, individual students came into my office to tell me they had decided that day of the memorial to commit their lives to Christ. Some of these collegians became part of our Sunday house-church group.

All of these events in our three years in Memphis undergirded my growing faith and dependence upon the Lord. More than ever, I realized that "He who calls you *is* faithful, who also will do *it*" (1 Thess. 5:24). God would always give us the strength we needed to accomplish any task He asked us to undertake.

God called us away from Memphis after a few years. We left behind the weekly contact we had with the kids who were part of that house church on Carr Avenue. However, they continued on as a community, and eventually most of them followed us into the Orthodox Church. Today that group is the community of St. John's Antiochian Orthodox Church. They bought an old Presbyterian church in mid-town Memphis and have had a remarkable growth and ministry in that area of the city. I first met the pastor and his wife when they were students at the University of Mississippi; they would often come up to Memphis on Sunday nights for our meetings.

In 2007, Marilyn and I had the joy of joining the people of St. John for their twentieth-anniversary celebration as an Orthodox Christian congregation. How grateful we were to see that the spiritual lives of each of these kids whom we knew as college students had matured and borne fruit. At this point they were not only married and parents but also, in many cases, they had become grandparents. Once again, God had proved His faithfulness and His promise that "My fruit will remain."

Satisfying as it was to minister in Memphis, by the end of our three years at the university, I was thirty-five years old and quite fatigued. I had been self-supporting since I was fifteen years old, and for twenty years I had worked incredibly hard, both through college and seminary, through our work in Campus Crusade, and now through my development stint at the university. By God's grace, I had tripled the private income of the school over that three-year period—but I was ready for a break.

CHAPTER 8

Grand Junction, Tennessee

"It is more blessed to give than to receive."

We had a friend in Memphis who was a real estate agent. One day, I asked him to be on the lookout for a little place in the country where we could go for an overnight and catch our breath. He told me about a pre-Civil War house in a little town called Grand Junction, an hour east of Memphis. The house was on the market for a mere five thousand dollars, since it had not been occupied for three years and the owner was desperate to unload it. Again, we recognized another diamond in the rough. With the money saved from the sale of our Evanston home, we bought the place for cash and restored the house, creating a really pretty pre-Civil War home.

The first night our family slept there was in March of 1972. We had moved enough mattresses and furniture in to accommodate our family of (by this time) seven people. I remember waking up on Saturday morning at about 5:30 a.m., as it was becoming light outside. The only sounds we could hear were the birds singing and a train going through town. I looked at Marilyn and she looked at me. "Would you like to live here?" I asked her.

"*Paupers' Alley*" – *Circa 1860*

THE GILLQUISTS · BOX 11 · GRAND JUNCTION, TENN. 38039

Drawing by Peter Gillquist

"Yes!" Marilyn immediately replied.

"Will our parents think we're crazy?" I said.

And she said, "I don't know, but I'd like to live here."

In June, I resigned my position at the university. By then, we had set enough money aside for me to take a year off just to be a husband and a dad. I told my friends that rather than wait until age sixty-five to retire, I was going to retire for one year at thirty-five, catch my breath, restore the house, and then rejoin the workforce. That year was one of our most wonderful years. Our sixth child, Peter Jon, joined the family, and we made the little place on Pauper's Alley into another one of our dream houses.

I know most people wouldn't have the luxury of doing what we did that year. We were able to make ends meet because we could grow our own food and had an incredibly low cost of living; among other things, the property taxes on the place were sixteen dollars a year. The inexpensive lifestyle enabled us to make it on next to nothing.

The highlight of our time in Grand Junction was the conversion of our county bootlegger, Mr. Fred.

In Grand Junction, there was a man who forever changed my life. I had purchased some land on the edge of town in the hopes of building a cabin on it one day. The land came with something the seller hadn't mentioned—a squatter. A mean old man lived in a rusted-out house trailer on the back border of the land. Everybody warned me, "Don't go near him, he's the meanest guy in town."

Mr. Fred, as he was called, had such a foul mouth that when he'd walk to town, women would walk on the other side of the street so they wouldn't have to hear him curse as he went by. Several people warned me, "Don't ever go near that trailer. He's got two mangy German Shepherd dogs and a sawed-off shotgun. He'll blow you away!"

Somehow God gave me a desire to try to reach this man and be his friend. One Sunday afternoon after church I said to my son Greg, who was twelve at the time, "Let's go out and meet Mr. Fred."

We walked the land together, and sure enough the dogs started barking. Mr. Fred came out with a shotgun, fortunately pointed down. I said, "Fred, I'm your neighbor. I want to meet you." We sat down and talked, the three of us.

Mr. Fred was seventy years old. He had been brought up in Texas, where he had murdered a man in a barroom fight. The marshal said, "I'll give you twenty-four hours to get out of town." So he came up to Tennessee, took a common-law wife, and had three children. By the time I met him, the woman had run off, and two of the three children were in jail. It was the biggest mess I'd ever seen in my life.

A short time after we met, Fred became very ill. He said to the grocer in town one day, "I know if I die, I'll go to hell." The grocer was able to talk with him about Jesus Christ, as I had done. But this time Mr. Fred was more open; he listened, and he committed himself to the Lord. I had the joy of baptizing him in Indian Creek outside of town a few weeks later.

This man was so socially inept that he could not handle a living room full of people. On Thanksgiving, for instance, we invited him to dinner. As soon as he arrived, he immediately went into our bedroom and stayed there. So at the end of the day, he and I and Greg together were a little church, as unbiblical as that might seem. We, as it were, took church to him.

Unlikely as it was, this man became one of the best friends I have ever had. When I was with him, I didn't have to say anything. He was totally undemanding. We moved him out of the trailer and helped him build a little house of his own on our land. I'd come home from a trip, hug my wife and kids, and go out there to sit by his stove for a spell and talk with him about the Lord.

Then he became ill again. I was scheduled to go to Alaska, and I knew I'd never see him on this earth again. Greg and I got in the car and drove to the hospital to say goodbye. I read him Revelation 21 and 22 about heaven. He said, "I could listen to this forever." I told him, "Fred, you'll not only listen to it forever, you'll live it forever." That was the last time I saw him.

Fred changed me. Here was a person who needed Jesus Christ and human friendship more than any man I've ever met, and I began to realize that there are people everywhere like that.

Everywhere. Nicholas Cabasilas wrote, "It is to function for Christ that the human heart has been created. Like an immense jewelry case, it is vast enough to contain even God! That is why nothing below can satisfy us."

A person with a speech impediment could have reached Fred. A Christian who knows almost nothing can always reach anyone like Mr. Fred, if he will just introduce him to Christ and be his friend. The world is full of the unsatisfied. They are our Orthodox vision for evangelism.

In addition to our friendship with Fred, we received other blessings in our time in Grand Junction. Again we formed a house-church that met in different homes of the people involved. Many of these people had been touched through the charismatic movement and had experienced the reality of the Holy Spirit in their lives, some for the very first time. Instead of the twenty-somethings we ministered to in Memphis, these folks were in their mid-forties and fifties and had grown up in the denominational churches of the area. They wanted something that was more Christ-centered and vital than they had experienced before.

The seven years in Grand Junction were significant; during that time, we moved as a community from a basic, spontaneous Sunday morning experience—albeit one centered still in the Eucharist—to a more liturgical worship style that expressed the fruit of our studies in early church history. As might be expected, our parishioners put up some strong resistance at first. Some of them had grown up in liturgical Protestant churches and believed liturgical worship was the problem, not the solution. Yet they were willing to give it another try.

After about a month of some fairly primitive early-Church liturgies, one of the most charismatic ladies in the group said, "You know, I like this now."

I said, "Why?"

"Because," she replied, "finally on Sunday mornings, we know where we're going, and that is to the Kingdom of God."

As the years went by, I reflected often on the fact that one way or another, all worship becomes liturgical. Even in a church that claims to be free of programmed worship, nonetheless, the same people sit in the same chairs on Sunday morning; the same guy prays the same prayer in the service on Sunday morning; the same person offers a sermon; essentially the same group of hymns are sung every Sunday. Worshippers move toward order instinctively.

During the Grand Junction years, we began to enter the beauty of the worship of the early Church. We now had a sense of entering into what our brothers and sisters in Christ over the two-thousand–year history of the Church had experienced in worship, rather than just making it up as we went along as eager twentieth-century seekers.

Even though the Grand Junction church was not able to stay together and come with us into the Orthodox Church, nonetheless we learned some marvelous lessons together, and we built some lasting friendships along the way.

CHAPTER 9

Our Greatest Blessing: The Six Bears

"Lord, we're all present and accounted for!"

By the time we left Grand Junction, we had six children—our six "bears"—and parenting became our major focus.

One of the great struggles we have today in the Church is that of preserving our children in the Orthodox Faith. Too often they lose interest. Can we somehow motivate our kids to be excited about following Christ and being Orthodox Christians? I believe there is a way. It takes commitment and hard work, but it's worth it.

As I related earlier, when I was about fourteen, I decided that if I were to have nothing else in life, I wanted a great marriage and family. I put it above education, above a successful career, above my standing in the community.

While we were students at the University of Minnesota, Dr. Bob Smith, a professor at Bethel College in St. Paul, gave a talk on marriage and the family. Somewhere during his talk, he created a picture that was indelibly etched in my mind. He said, "One day I'm going to stand before the judgment seat of Christ as a father,

The Gillquist family in 1976

and my goal is to have my wife and children by my side, saying, 'Lord, we're all present and accounted for. Here's Mary, here's Steve, here's Johnny—we're all here.'"

That night, I prayed, "Lord, that's what I want when I get married and have children—that we might all enter Your eternal Kingdom intact."

Through college, seminary, and forty-five years of marriage, my commitment to have a great family and to bring them into the Kingdom with me has never wavered. My wife and I have kept our marriage healthy and have striven to be godly parents and grandparents. There are five specific things Marilyn and I tried to do and, by the grace of God, mostly succeeded in doing to build up our family in Christ and His Church.

1. Make Your Family Your Priority

After the Kingdom of God, our families should be our highest priority. If we're going to raise Orthodox Christian families, our spouses and children have to be at the top of the list, after Christ and His Church.

Of course, for Orthodox Christians, our journey with Christ and His Church always comes first. On that matter, the Scriptures are clear, the Fathers are clear, and the Liturgy is clear. At least four times each Sunday morning we call to mind our holy and blessed God-bearer and all the saints, saying, "Let us commit ourselves and each other and all our life to Christ our God."

After this, however, our call is to prioritize our families above our jobs, our social lives, and all the things that vie for our time.

At each juncture in my life, I have always fought a battle for work-versus-family balance. I wish I could say that maintaining the right balance is easy, but it's not. Many of our Christian friends and acquaintances have lost their families because, by their own admission, their careers came first. They were absentee dads and moms, and their jobs ate them up.

In most of my work over the years, I've traveled. Some years, I've been gone about half of the 365 days. So when the airlines some years back started offering frequent flyer miles, I thought, "Wait a minute, here's a way to benefit from these programs—I can take my kids along!"

I began to take one child at a time with me on some of my trips. On a trip out East with one of my daughters, we rented a car in New York City and drove to Harrisburg, Pennsylvania. I think we had the most meaningful conversation ever during that drive. Another time I had to drive all night from Chicago to Atlanta, and my son Greg traveled with me. When we got out into the country where there were no city lights, he remarked he could see the stars more clearly than he had ever seen them before. That night we talked about God's creation. As adults, most all our six children have said, "Dad, some of my favorite times were those trips I got to take with you."

If you're busy, find a way to compensate. I made appointments with my children. If your time is in heavy demand and you don't block out time for the kids, you'll never see them. If someone calls and has to see you, you say, "You know, Joe, I've got an appointment. I can see you tomorrow." Make a decision to prioritize your family.

2. Tell Your Children of God's Faithfulness

In Deuteronomy 4, Moses is talking to the children of Israel about the importance of keeping God's commandments. Then he speaks directly to parents and grandparents: "Only take heed to yourself, and diligently keep yourself, lest you forget the things your eyes have seen, and lest they depart from your heart all the days of your life. And teach them to your children and your grandchildren" (Deut. 4:9 NKJV).

Maybe you are a parent who came to Christ later in life and you feel you didn't do a good job spiritually with your kids, and now they have families of their own. Well, now you've got a crack at your grandkids! This opportunity does not mean you become your grandchildren's parent. But what you can do is tell those grandchildren what God has done for you, just like Moses says. Talk to them. If you've become more dedicated to Christ later in life, tell your grandkids about that. Tell them lessons you've learned. Tell them real-life stories about God's faithfulness and His mercy to you.

Moses goes on to explain the importance of such conversations by recalling what the Lord had said to him: "that they may learn to fear Me all the days they live on the earth, and *that* they may teach their children" (Deut. 4:10 NKJV). Children who are rightly taught the Word of God will teach their own children.

How did we teach our kids? Before I answer, let me say I think it's possible to overdo it. You can't ram Christianity down your family's throats. If you are a zealot, you may be tempted to force-feed them until they become rebels. I met a few men in seminary who were there not because they wanted to be, or even because God had called them; rather, they came to please their parents, and that's scary.

Central to everything we tried to do as a family was going to church Sunday morning. Even through the struggles of the teenage years, there was never a question as to what we did Sunday morning. I was not a priest when our older children were teenagers, but regardless of that, as a family we were in church on Sunday morning. If we traveled, we went to church wherever we were.

I knew that if I cut corners with our kids, they would cut corners with theirs. If you compromise, they will compromise more. So this point was never open for discussion.

Orthodox churches host many services. So what did we do? We always went to Saturday night Vespers, Sunday morning Liturgy, and major feast days. Was there mercy in that? Absolutely. Would I keep them away from the prom or a big football game on Saturday night? No. But we didn't want them to be out so late that it interfered with their participation on Sunday morning. On feast days, if they had a midterm the next day, did I force them to go? I did not. The line I tried to walk was to put Christ and the Church first, but not to do it with a hammerlock. There was discipline, and there was also mercy.

That is the same spirit we tried to keep in family prayer. When the kids were little, we read Bible stories to them every night. We prayed together. Then as they got older we encouraged them to say their own prayers at night.

In becoming Orthodox, we graduated into the church calendar. During Advent and Lent, the Lexicon specifies scriptural readings from the Old and New Testaments. At the dinner table during those seasons, we would do those readings together every night. When I was home, I would read and comment on the passage. We would talk about how the passage related to our lives and how it related to Lent or Advent. When I was on the road, I would ask someone else to fill that role. That way the family was on the spiritual diet the Church prescribes during those two seasons.

Then the rest of the year, I would give the blessing for the food, and often the conversation at the dinner table would focus on Christ. If the kids had questions, I would discuss the Scriptures with them. The rhythm of the church year provided us with the framework for our family life too.

3. Love Your Spouse

Thirdly—and I can't stress this enough—we do our kids a favor when we love our spouses. Psychologists tell us that even more important than a child feeling love from parents is for that child to know mom and dad love each other. Kids know instinctively that if love in marriage breaks down, there's not much left over for them.

The beautiful passage that describes this love is in Ephesians 5. It's the passage we read as the epistle at our Orthodox weddings. "Husbands, love your wives, just as Christ also loved the church" (v. 25). That means that we love our wives enough to die for them. We martyr ourselves to each other; that's what the wedding crowns are about. I love my wife more than life itself.

The crowns also speak of royalty. In my homily at the marriage of our younger son, I said, "Peter, treat her like a queen! Kristina, treat him like a king!" That arrangement always works out really well.

I don't think we should ever stop courting our spouses. Marilyn and I still go out on dates, and we've been married forty-five years. Sometimes you just need to take a break from life's routine, go out together, talk and listen, and remind yourself of why you fell in love.

Before I got married, I had a friend who had a great relationship with his wife. I asked, "What's your secret?" His advice: "Find out what she likes to do and do it." Marilyn likes to shop. In our early years we couldn't afford anything, so we'd go out window-shopping after the stores closed.

Now, if I've got a day free, I ask her, "What do you want to do, honey?"

She usually answers, "Let's go shopping."

So I'll put on a sport shirt, drive downtown, hold her hand as we look in the windows, and buy the grandkids a gift. Grow in your love and keep up the courtship.

4. Never Discipline out of Anger

There are times when things go wrong, even badly wrong. I would love to tell you that none of our six kids ever missed a beat or that we were infallible. But there isn't a family alive that is free of tension and difficulty. On a sliding scale, three of our children were relatively easy to bring up, and three were more challenging. When some of them got stubborn in their teenage years, I would say to Marilyn, "Remember what we were like at that age? They're no different." I was difficult as a teenager, and some of that showed up in our kids.

Saint John the Apostle said, "I have no greater joy than to hear that my children walk in truth" (3 John 4). The opposite of that is also true. There is no greater heartache than when our children do not walk in truth. We've had a few big bumps in our family. There were nights my wife and I were both in tears as we tried to sleep. We would say, "Lord, is there light at the end of this tunnel?"

One of the verses I memorized out of the Old Testament early in my own parenthood was Proverbs 22:6 (NKJV):

> *Train up a child in the way he should go,*
> *And when he is old he will not depart from it.*

Let me assure you, that promise from God is true. There were days I wondered whether our family would stand before the Lord fully intact. Thank God for repentance, forgiveness, restoration, and grace.

Immediately after St. Paul's exhortation on marriage in Ephesians 5, he continues with parent-child relationships. "Children, obey your parents in the Lord, for this is right. 'Honor your father and mother,' which is the first commandment with promise: 'that it may be well with you and you may live long on the earth'" (Eph. 6:1–3). This is another dependable promise. If a child obeys his parents, he'll live a longer life. So we train them up to be obedient.

It is helpful now and then to sit down with our children and remind them why it's so important to obey mom and dad: simply put, if children do not learn to obey their parents, they will not learn to obey God. The consequences of that disobedience are dire, both in this life and the next. So one reason we obey mom and dad is that in turn we learn to follow the Lord.

The next verse gives the other side of the coin: "Fathers, do not provoke your children to wrath, but bring them up in the training and admonition of the Lord" (Eph. 6:4). I don't know where I got this idea (few things I do are original), but when I had to correct our girls, I would hold their hand. In my early days as a dad, I would sit them in a chair and then sit across from them. But one day I said to myself, "This doesn't say what I want to say." So I would sit with them on the couch, hold their hand, look them in the eye, and tell them what I wanted them to do.

Two of my daughters have come to me independently as adults and thanked me for holding their hands when I corrected them. They both had friends whose dads embarrassed their daughters, disciplining in a way that was probably too strong. I encourage fathers to guard against a discipline or correction that engenders wrath in your children. After the correction, give them a hug and let them know you love them. There are times when a father may need to refrain from discipline on the spot because he is angry. Remember that line from *The Incredible Hulk*? "You won't like me when I'm angry." If that's true for a cartoon character, how much more is it true for a real-life dad?

Like any couple, Marilyn and I started out very idealistically, saying to each other, "When it comes to raising kids, we're going to do it right, and if we do it right from the very start, there will be no problems. There will be no use of free will on the part of the kids, because we'll lay the foundation and they'll never miss a beat." The fact is, rarely is that true.

Three of the kids probably cannot tell of a time when they did not believe or love Jesus Christ, and three of the kids were strugglers. When Marilyn and I would talk about the strugglers, we had to remind ourselves that those three kids were like us. We struggled; we were not those who never missed a beat, but we were those who called a lot of what we were taught in our churches and in our homes into question. Therefore, we needed to understand the strugglers rather than worry about them; instead, we prayed for them.

One year it was the Fourth of July, and one of our daughters who had struggled with me was traveling with me in New York City. I think it was her first time there, and she was so excited to be in, arguably, the great fashion and entertainment center of America. On the morning of July 4, we asked the concierge at the hotel, "What's the best fireworks display in New York?"

"Without question, it's Battery Park, which is on the south end of Manhattan," he said. "It's that part of the island that overlooks the Statue of Liberty. As you watch the fireworks display in the sky, you see the outline of the Statue of Liberty illumined below. But here's the thing: you've got to get there early, because once that area fills up, they cordon it off and they won't let anybody else in. So mark my words: be sure to get there early."

We arrived sometime in the late afternoon, realizing that it would probably be dark enough around nine or nine-thirty for the fireworks to begin. What we didn't realize was what all the rest of the natives there knew, and that is that you bring a picnic lunch and a couple of those fold-out aluminum-tubing chairs with the mesh ribbons so you don't have to stand for five hours before the fireworks display starts.

By nine o'clock, both of us were dying of hunger and wracked with back pain, having stood on the cement walk of Battery Park waiting for the show to begin. At about nine-thirty, the first of the fireworks went off, and it was the most spectacular Fourth of July fireworks display that either of us had ever seen. At one point, our daughter turned to me and said, "Dad, remind me never again to complain about standing for the Divine Liturgy, or that it's too long. If I can stand all this time for the United States of America, certainly I can stand an hour and a half each week for the Kingdom of God." And the fact is, she got it right.

5. Help Your Children Discern God's Will

Let's look again at Proverbs 22:6: "Train up a child in the way he should go, and when he is old he will not depart from it." The phrase, "in the way he should go," is not speaking of the way you want him to go. Rather, it's the way God wants him to go. In other words, taking into account that child's gifts, his emotional makeup, his personality, his intellect, his calling, you help him discern the path God has for him.

I'm really pleased that Peter Jon is a priest and that Wendy's husband is an Orthodox deacon. But I'm equally pleased with

Greg, who is a marketing guy, and with Terri, who is a mom of five, and with Ginger and Heidi, who both work outside the home to help their husbands provide for their children.

To repeat, our job as parents is to try to discern with our children what God wants them to do and then train them in that way. Whether their calling is in business or law or retailing or service to the Church, I want them to be the best they can be, for the glory of God. All of us are in the ministry of Christ by virtue of our baptism. We are ordained as His servants, lay and clergy both. Therefore, whatever we do, our goal is to do it for the glory of God.

Thank God, these measures produced good fruit. At our stage in life, it is wonderful with just the two of us at home to think back over the years and to thank the Lord for children, spouses, and grandchildren who are faithful. There is nothing like it.

That doesn't mean there will never be any more problems. I'm naïve, but not naïve enough to believe that. There may be bumps yet to come. But as we confess at our weddings, "The prayers of parents establish the foundations of houses." These years are not kickback time, but they are a time of thanksgiving.

Later in our lives as a family, we moved from Tennessee to California. Marilyn and I were going through the house to determine what to take and what to leave behind. The home we'd bought out west in Santa Barbara was barely large enough for our family; the rooms were small, and the configuration of the house was vastly different from that of our pre-Civil War place in western Tennessee. I remember walking into the kitchen and looking at our beautiful round oak table with beautiful pedestal-and-scroll legs, where all eight of us could gather for a meal together.

I had bought the table off the back of a pickup truck for less than fifty dollars. It was covered in white enamel paint, so I stripped and refinished it. It had two leaves to expand it, which in those days was a rarity for an antique table. Once I fixed it up, it was a beautiful addition to our nice, big country kitchen.

I said to Marilyn, who hadn't seen the California house yet, "There's no way this table will fit in any room in our new home. We'll need to find a place for it or get rid of it."

Our daughter Terri, who was about twelve at the time, overheard me. Ever since she was about four years old, Terri would say to us repeatedly, "Mom and Dad, all I ever want to do is grow up, get married, and have a lot of children." She was an incredible caregiver for her younger brother and sister, and was always mommy's helper and domestic assistant.

"Dad," she said, "as far back as I can remember, I always pictured that when I got married and had children, our family would sit around this table like all of us do now."

I blinked back the tears and said to Marilyn, "Let's load it on the truck."

When we arrived in Santa Barbara, one of the first things I asked the parish pastor, Fr. Richard Ballew, was, "Is there anybody within the church who is in need of a dining room table?"

He said, "As a matter of fact, the Speier family is."

The Speiers lived in a house just down the street from us and had no dining room table. I explained to Fr. Nicholas and Jan that if they would like our table, it was theirs to use for the next several years, but our daughter Terri had laid claim to it and wanted to use it after she was married.

In one of those serendipitous moments that seem to happen periodically in our lives, not only did Terri get married and claim the table, she married Scott Speier! So as Scott left his home, he brought the table with him to his new home with Terri. Today if you visit the Speiers in Santa Barbara, you'll walk into a beautiful living room and through a doorway to a combined kitchen and family room. Right there in the center of the whole thing is this beautiful round oak table with both leaves in it and eight or ten chairs around it. Every night the Speier family and any guests who may have joined them enjoy a meal around Terri's childhood table.

CHAPTER 10

Hello. I'm Johnny Cash.

"You're the one to write the story."

After my sabbatical year in Grand Junction, where I spent quality time with my six children, I began to ask God for my next step, knowing that one can't coast forever without a monthly income. Again, God revealed to us His mercy in a completely unexpected way.

The phone rang one morning, and it was the editor of Zondervan Publishers. Bob asked me, "Would you, by chance, be available for a writing assignment that would keep you busy for a year?" I replied that I would and asked him to tell me about it. He said, "It's a big Christian celebrity book."

"Who is it?"

"I can't tell you until the contract is signed, but that should be done within a week or two. I simply want to know if you're available, because, in our opinion, you're the one to write the story."

I said, "I'm available, but I certainly want to meet the person and make sure the chemistry is right between us, and that this person is sincere as a Christian."

Bob said, "Give me a week or two, and I'll call you back."

Bob called about ten days later and asked, "Are you ready?"

"Yes."

He said, "It's Johnny Cash."

"You're kidding me."

Johnny Cash was a legend, and his music was inextricably linked with my youth. I can still remember driving down Hennepin Avenue in Minneapolis as a high school student with the car radio on and hearing him sing "I'll Walk the Line." I thought to myself, "What a voice!" He was the equal of other great contemporaries like Elvis Presley, Carl Perkins, and Jerry Lee Lewis.

Though I was never a great fan of country music per se, how on earth do you not like the voice and music of Johnny Cash?

So I said, "I want to meet him."

Bob said, "I've already arranged for that, and we'd like you to fly into Nashville in a week or so. I'll meet you there, and we'll go out to his home and make sure this whole thing is a match."

Later, people would ask me, "Why is it that Zondervan tapped you to be the writer for Johnny Cash?"

I suppose this might be the answer: By the time that phone call came, I had written three books for Zondervan, two of which had become bestsellers in the Christian booksellers' market. The first book was entitled *Love Is Now*, a spiritual guidebook for youth in the Jesus Movement. In it, I described God's powerful love and the forgiveness available through Jesus Christ. It was a book written in the *lingua franca* of the younger set, and before long half a million copies were in print. People living legalistic and defeated Christian lives would tell me the book was liberating for them.

The second bestseller was written to address the controversy and confusion surrounding the charismatic and Pentecostal movements, and I entitled it *Let's Quit Fighting About the Holy Spirit*. It was one of a few books during that time that offered a middle-ground position: on the one hand, I confessed that the gifts of the Holy Spirit were present, not only in the New Testament, but really throughout the history of the Church. On the other hand, I sounded a warning about the excesses and high-pressure tactics employed by some charismatic Christian leaders. The book struck a chord with both sides of the charismatic debate and also stated the Orthodox Christian view of the work of the Holy Spirit, even though we weren't yet Orthodox. I still have people who thank me for taking a balanced look at the work of the Holy Spirit among the people of God.

So on the one hand, Zondervan knew me as a proven author. Also, for four years I had lived in Tennessee, the home state of Johnny Cash. I assumed the Zondervan people figured that I knew the culture of Southern Christians and could relate to country musicians. I counted it an honor to be asked to do the book. Later, it turned out that I was well compensated for my efforts; but what they didn't know at Zondervan is that I would have done the book for free!

Interestingly enough, on the flight from Memphis to Nashville I sat next to a man who was a well-known hospital administrator in Memphis. I had helped the man's son become a Christian, and so we began a conversation. One thing led to another, and he ended up offering me a job as a development officer at the hospital, a job that would be similar to my University of Memphis post. It felt odd to say, "Henry, I'm sorry to say no, but I think I'm committed for the next year to do a project that is of great interest to me."

He said, "What's that?"

I said, "It's writing the life story of Johnny Cash!"

I do not want to "big time" this man, I thought immediately. Yet I felt I needed to shoot straight with him. After our flight, as Henry and I walked from the gate to the main terminal, Johnny Cash's chauffeur was waiting for me near the door. Henry watched me get into the back of a long, black Rolls Royce and motor off to Johnny Cash's suburban Nashville home.

After we turned off the main highway toward the Cash home, the chauffeur said to me, "Look all around you at the surrounding land; Mr. Cash owns all of this." He went on to tell me how grateful he was to Johnny for bringing him to faith in Jesus Christ. My heart was very encouraged by this beginning.

As we pulled up into the Cash compound, I thought, "How am I going to introduce myself to him? If it's going to be 'Mr. Cash' and 'Mr. Gillquist,' I don't think this relationship will work." So I determined that when we walked through the back stairs on the main level up into the house itself, I would reach out my hand and say, "Hi, brother," because I wanted to relate to him as a brother in Jesus Christ.

I stepped inside the house, and there stood the legendary singer at the top of the stairs. As I reached the landing, I held out my hand and said, "Hi, brother."

He said, "Hi, brother," and I knew it was a match.

Johnny's purpose in writing the book titled *Man in Black* (published in 1975) was to tell his story in his own words. His remarkable conversion from a life of drugs and debauchery, sadly so common in the world of entertainment, led him to become an outspoken Christian who brought Jesus Christ into the very center of his country music career. He told me he'd decided to "tithe" his music—in every concert he performed, be it in front of a secular or Christian audience, he always made sure that ten percent of his music reflected the Gospel of Jesus Christ. Many of these were the old-time gospel songs we've come to love, such as "Praise the Lord, I Saw the Light" and "Daddy Sang Bass," and many were songs he had written, such as "Over the Next Hill and We'll be Home."

At Johnny's request, we worked on the book at the Cash home in Jamaica, a grand mansion they had bought and beautified. It was built in the 1700s and was the great house of a sugar plantation that covered numerous acres. Built with imported Japanese maple framing, the house had a huge windbreak on the southeast side that had served to deflect Lord-knows-how-many hurricanes over the 250 years that had elapsed between the construction of the house and the year we spent working there together on Johnny's book.

I'll never forget our first evening in the Jamaica home. The Zondervan editor had also flown in to help me launch the interviews. We were ushered into a beautiful dining room with a table that must have been able to seat two dozen people. The dinner guests that night were essentially Bob and myself and Johnny and his family. I remember trying to decide what to wear for dinner. Bob said, "I'm going to wear a coat but no tie," and I decided to do the same. I remember Johnny walked in wearing a black shirt, black slacks, and bare feet.

We sat down together, and Johnny asked Bob to pray. The bill of fare was T-bone steaks, some great vegetables, and a salad the cook had made and served. From my high school etiquette class

I remembered that I should wait for the lady of the house to pick up her fork to take a bite; but before June had a chance to eat, John had picked up his T-bone with his fingers and started in. The pressure for following any etiquette manual was off.

We spent a week together recording the first several chapters of the book. At John's request, I had bought a cassette-tape player that was quite sophisticated for that era—battery-operated, with a great microphone. I also bought a box of ninety-minute cassette tapes. Sometimes we'd sit on the porch and he would dictate his story; other times he liked to walk in the woods surrounding the home and dictate. My goal was to get the whole thing on tape and have it transcribed, then create paragraphs and chapters. His job would be to look over the final draft and make any changes he wished to make.

There were a couple of very powerful moments during those two one-week interviews in Jamaica. One time when Bob and I were riding with Johnny in his Land Rover, he began to open up his heart. He knew that Jesus Christ had become his Savior and Lord, and yet he was fearful of the great judgment seat of Christ because of all the sins he had committed in his previous life.

I looked at Bob and he looked at me, and we said, "Who gets to go first?"

That day we were able to explain to John the incredible grace of God and the work of Christ on the Cross to forgive the sins we had committed, past, present, and future. This might have been the first time John realized the totality of God's mercy. He began to comprehend that whether voluntary or involuntary, in word and in deed, in knowledge or in ignorance, those sins that he and we had committed in the years of our youth were as nailed to the cross as anything we had done since our conversion. It was a day I would never forget.

The second highlight of the interviews was the time when we were sitting on the porch of that beautiful home in Jamaica, that great house, and John was revisiting his memories of his first marriage to Vivian and the subsequent birth of their four daughters. Those were years he was hooked on alcohol and drugs and all the things that often accompany life on the road. At one point, he broke down in tears and asked June to come out on the porch. She came up to him and hugged him, and he said, "Honey, for the first time in my life, I've taken the blame for my failure in my first marriage." Again, it was a moment I'll never forget, as the gift of repentance was that day given to him for his shortcomings as a husband and father in a marriage that ultimately failed.

The book was destined to be a bestseller from the start. Johnny was at the very height of his career. Evangelical Christians knew he had been converted. Billy Graham had asked him and June to give their testimonies at some of his crusades in states down South; he was witnessing to Christ in television appearances. I said to my Zondervan friends, "You guys can print this book on toilet paper and it'll sell a million." We knew we had a winner.

When the book was launched in Nashville in the fall of 1975, Marilyn and I were asked to come up for the celebration of the publication, held at Johnny's beautiful recording studios outside of Nashville, called the House of Cash. My own parents were taken with the fact that I had been asked to be the ghostwriter for the book, and my stepmom said, "Do you think there's any chance your dad and I could come to the celebration?"

I said, "I'd love to have you there! Let me ask."

Without hesitation, John said, "Absolutely." So it was a joy for me to have not only my own wife present, but also my parents, who had driven down from Minnesota to be present at this celebration. My mom still has the picture of her and dad posing with Johnny Cash at the reception.

Thus it turned out that my year of moving back into the working world was one of the most exciting of my life. In preparation for writing the book, I accompanied Johnny and his family on two special tours, one in the Houston, Texas, area, and an even more memorable book tour in and around Johnstown, Pennsylvania, where a hard-core base of his fans lived.

In Pennsylvania, Johnny held a show in the Johnstown Armory. We had stayed in what was then the nicest hotel in town, the Sheraton. Johnstown is of course famous for the tragic flood of 1889. As you walked in the front door of the Sheraton, there was a long hallway flanked on the left by a registration desk and on the right by a restaurant and lounge. At the end of the hall were an elevator and a huge set of stairs going up to the second floor.

I rode with John and his family to the concert just a few blocks away at the Armory that evening, but after the concert was over, June and the kids went back to the hotel, and John asked if I'd remain with him while he closed up with his band; then we could ride back to the hotel together.

About a half-hour after the concert was over, the limousine pulled back up to the stage door, and John and I went out and got in the car. It was a very cold night. Of course, he would always wear black for the concerts, and his winter coat was a huge black cape with a red satin lining. He looked like a stunning country version of Superman, with that cape and long, jet-black hair.

As we got out of the car and walked into the hotel headed toward the back of that elongated lobby, we could hear three middle-aged women in the lounge (who had probably had a little too much to drink) scream, "There he is!"

John said, "Let's go!"

Though I had lettered two years in track in high school, I could barely keep up with him as we ran down this extended lobby with these three gals coming out of the lounge trying to catch us. John said, "Forget the elevator. We're taking the stairs." We took them two and three stairs at a time and reached the top landing on the second floor. The women were on their way up in hot pursuit. He reached in his pocket, got his hotel key, put it in the door of his suite, and he said, "Get in here."

We opened the door, practically fell into the room, and he slammed the door behind us. I felt embarrassed because June had already gone to bed, and here I was, standing in their bedroom. John walked over and called the hotel desk and asked security to get the ladies out of there. When the coast was clear, about ten minutes later, I walked back to my room down the hall.

As I returned to the blessed privacy of my own room, I couldn't help but reflect on the price that entertainers like Johnny Cash pay. What looks like glamour and glitter from a distance really amounts to a total loss of privacy and freedom of movement.

As a Christian, Johnny was more than willing to pay this price for an opportunity to represent Jesus Christ on the country music circuit. There were many people he touched in the course of his career, such as the prisoner at Folsom Prison who said, "When John gave the concert, that was the day I met Jesus Christ in his Johnny-Cash form." This incarcerated man went on to be a very strong believer, as did many of the others Johnny touched along the way.

After the year of working on *Man in Black*, I realized I relished the experience, along with the many other things I'd worked on in my twenties and thirties. *I hope I don't settle into some boring career that puts food on the table and little else,* I thought on more than one occasion in those years. I would not have traded those years spent serving the Lord in a variety of ways for anything: whether it was on college campuses, with the counter-culture people in Memphis, with the country people of Grand Junction, or now with one of the most faithful Christians in the music business.

CHAPTER 11

Thomas Nelson and Publishing

"Sam, where do you buy your clothes?"

One Sunday our family was in Nashville as I was winding up my work on the Johnny Cash book. I was giving the sermon at a church founded by my dear friend Gordon Walker, one of our former Campus Crusade associates studying the early Church with us.

This was 1975, and we were still in the very earliest stages of discovering the Orthodox Christian faith. That morning the service consisted of country music songs, a forty-five–minute Bible-exposition sermon, and then the serving of communion. A visiting Orthodox Christian would not have recognized the service as being in any way Orthodox; on the other hand, an Evangelical Protestant visitor might say, "This is a little more liturgical than what is done at my church."

After the service, a member of the church approached me. His name was Frank, and he worked for the well-known Christian publisher, Thomas Nelson. He said, "We just lost our book editor, and I would like you to keep an eye out for us as to whom we could hire to replace him."

I said, "Tell me what you're looking for."

"We would like someone with seminary training, someone who is good at administrative work, someone who has done journalism, and someone who has written and edited books. We want someone who believes the Bible and who is sensitive about presenting the Christian message in terms that lay readers can understand."

So I said, "I'll keep my eyes open for you."

Later that day, driving home on I-40 from Memphis to Jackson and on to Grand Junction, I thought to myself, "The guy described me!" When I got home, I called my friend Gordon Walker back and told him what Frank had said. "What would you think if I applied for the job?" I asked him.

He said, "I think you ought to. Let me have Frank call you." Before I knew it, an interview appointment was set up with Sam Moore, who was the president of Nelson.

During my three years at the university, I had worn a coat and tie to work every day. Part of the fun in moving to Grand Junction was that I had no need to wear a coat and tie; in fact, I gave away my suits to a public school teacher in a neighboring town who was in need of a decent wardrobe. So when I took the interview with Sam, who himself is a very natty dresser, I showed up in a country-cut jacket with a pair of bellbottoms that were all the rage at that time, rounded out by cowboy boots. I walked into his office and noticed that he cased me from head to foot and then back up to my head again. This was not the typical dress of a Thomas Nelson executive!

The interview went extremely well, and obviously my success as the writer for Johnny Cash's book, *Man in Black*, played no small role in Sam's interest in hiring me. My Dallas Seminary and Wheaton Graduate School credentials didn't hurt a bit, as Sam was very committed to the authority and the inspiration of the Scriptures. My years at the University of Memphis were a real plus since I'd worked in an administrative post there, and this gave him the confidence that I would know how to manage a department.

Toward the end of the interview, Sam leaned forward in his chair and said, "Peter, are you willing to put the company first?"

I said, "Sam, you're a Christian, and you know that would be idolatry."

"What do you mean?" he asked, a bit puzzled.

I said, "For us as Christians, we put Christ and His Kingdom first. Jesus told us, 'Seek first the kingdom of God and its righteousness,'" I said. "Then as Christian men, we put our wives and our families second." We both shared a high-profile friend working for another publisher who held the job that I was interviewing for at Nelson; his wife had left him for another man, explaining, "He was never home." So I said, "Sam, one of the earmarks of my own life is that I've never been willing to sacrifice my family on the altar of success in business or any profession."

Then I said, "I am willing to put the company third, and my commitment is to work my tail off for you."

He said, "You've got the job."

Then he said, "Peter, here at the company, we will need you to dress more traditionally than you're dressed today."

I told him, "No problem," and recounted the story of giving

away my suits to a friend. "Sam, where do you buy your clothes?" I asked. He said at Levy's, and I replied, "Who do you deal with?" and he gave me the name of the salesman. "I'll stop there tomorrow and restock up on business suits," I promised.

We agreed on a salary, and then I said something to Sam I hoped he would understand. "I'm involved with a group of former

Peter during the Thomas Nelson years

Campus Crusade colleagues. We're on a spiritual journey to find the Church of the New Testament in its twentieth-century expression. Knowing your own story, as one who came from Lebanon and was baptized in the Orthodox faith, we're pretty sure that the church we're going to end up with is the Orthodox Church. What I'd like to do is to take a twenty-five–percent salary cut and work for you three-fourths time. The other one-fourth of the year I'd like to join my colleagues in studying the faith of the early Church. I know this is not the typical way to run the book-procurement end of a company, but I know I can handle it because I've been able to make many contacts in Christian communities through my work in the last ten years."

We agreed that I would do the job for two years. Sam would not fire me, and I would not quit; furthermore, I would do everything I could to put the book program at Thomas Nelson on the map.

Some of my friends in the publishing world were curious that I had signed on to work with Thomas Nelson as opposed to other established Evangelical publishers. The truth is, part of the joy of my life has always been doing "turnarounds." I always preferred working in virgin territory rather than walking on an easy and established path.

Thomas Nelson fit that description. A 200-year-old company started by a Christian man intent on publishing Christian classics and the Bible at prices common people could afford, Thomas Nelson had morphed into being rather secular in its outlook, operating from a profit motive rather than a ministry motive. When Sam bought the company in 1969, his goal was to make it into the most outstanding Christian publisher in the world, a lofty goal and a herculean task. By the time I came on board, it was the number-one Bible publisher in the world, bigger than numbers two, three, and four put together. My job was to bring it back to its Evangelical publishing roots.

At the end of two years, I loved my work and Sam was pleased with the progress we had made. What began as a two-year commitment turned into eleven years of service filled with much joy. Not only were we able to identify and publish fine new talent in the Christian world, such as Charles Swindoll, Jack Sparks, Jody and Linda Dillow, and Sally and Don Meredith, but we also signed on notable established authors as well.

As an immigrant American, Sam was as eager as I was to publish Christians from various ethnic and minority communities. For instance, I met a remarkable African-American woman named Frances Kelley. The anchor for *Good Morning Memphis* on the ABC network affiliate, she was also a ticket agent for American Airlines at the Memphis International Airport. Because I was flying in and out of Memphis so much, we became good friends. Frances had one of the most amazing stories I'd ever heard, and we eventually published it under the title *Better Than I Was.* When Billy Graham held his crusade in Memphis in 1978, she was one of the local people asked to give her testimony in the Liberty Bowl stadium. Even though books published by unknown minority authors did not usually sell at the same rate as those written by experienced writers, we were gratified that Nelson helped establish the careers of several outstanding authors like Frances.

After I took the job at Nelson, people sometimes pulled me aside to tell me how difficult it was working for Sam Moore. An immigrant from Beirut, Lebanon, Sam managed his employees with what we would call a more Middle-Eastern style of leadership. In the Lebanese culture, the boss is the boss, and what he says goes, and I had learned to adjust to that. Someone tipped me off early on that the number-one characteristic a Lebanese leader often values in his employees is not super-productivity, but loyalty.

Sam was an incredibly compassionate man, and so it was easy for me to be loyal to him. I deeply admired his character, his vision, and his willingness to put Christ first in everything he did. By both his assessment and mine, I was one of the few employees who, thank God, never crossed swords with him.

One time Sam called me into his office and asked me to recruit an author I did not feel comfortable with. I knew that at the end of the day he called the shots, so I said, "Sam, would you give me ten minutes to try to talk you out of this? If at the end of that time you still want me to go meet this person, I'll be on the plane in the morning."

He said, "Fine."

I then explained how the author he had in mind would not be acceptable to many of the other proven authors on our list, and I went through the reasons why. As I finished making my case, he thanked me and said, "That's fine. Don't go!"

During my tenure at Thomas Nelson, I was often on the road recruiting new authors. This also gave me the opportunity to meet American Orthodox leaders in the cities I visited. One of the first Greek Orthodox bishops I met, while on business in Pittsburgh, was Bishop Maximos. Though an immigrant, His Grace had gained a deep and comprehensive understanding of American Evangelicals and had been involved in many dialogues with Protestant leaders in Pittsburgh.

Many people urged me to meet him. On this particular visit,

he invited me for lunch and graciously invited me to give the blessing for the food, even though Orthodox protocol would dictate otherwise. I knew that in the Orthodox Church there were familiar prayers of blessing that people used, but I had no idea what they were; I offered my typical, spontaneous Protestant prayer and was deeply moved by his openness and humility as he accepted my prayer and thanked me for it.

Even though we didn't enter the Orthodox Church through the Greek Archdiocese, nonetheless Bishop Maximos and I maintained our friendship. I am so grateful for the role he played in introducing us to the Church. It was through his encouragement that I also met Metropolitan Christopher of the Serbian Orthodox Church on that same visit to Pittsburgh.

Another blessing of working for Sam Moore at Thomas Nelson was that he understood our desire to become Orthodox and was very supportive of it, even though he himself was immersed in the Protestant Evangelical world. "I never left the Orthodox Church," he told me one day. "I simply gravitated more and more into the Evangelical Christian world." In fact, when Sam's mother passed away in Nashville, I attended her wake the night before her funeral. It was the first time in my life I had ever prayed for a departed soul. Marie Ziady lived and died a faithful Orthodox Christian.

Years later, after I had resigned from Nelson to work full-time for the Antiochian Archdiocese, I had the great joy of introducing Sam to Metropolitan Philip. The Metropolitan was in Nashville to receive into the Church one of our seeker communities, the parish that became St. Ignatius of Antioch in suburban Franklin, Tennessee. Sam and his wife Peggy hosted a private dinner for Metropolitan Philip and his assistant, Archdeacon Hans, to which Fr. Gordon Walker and I were invited. It was so enjoyable to sit back and watch them carry on a conversation in Arabic. They were born about a year apart from each other in Lebanon, and we discovered that one of Sam's teachers later became Patriarch Ignatius IV of Antioch. When Sam and Peggy later traveled to Lebanon, Sam was able to visit his former high school teacher, now the patriarch, and rekindle that connection.

So the years at Nelson not only were wonderful years of involvement in Christian publishing, but they also taught me how to work for a man from the Middle East, which I would continue to do under the leadership of Metropolitan Philip in the Antiochian Archdiocese in the years to come.

Shortly after I arrived at Nelson, I was in the office one day and met two gentlemen who had just been hired to be president and vice president of my division, Bob Wolgemuth and Michael Hyatt. I was to be reporting to Mike, and if my memory serves me correctly, Mike asked if I would be available to go out to lunch on his first day on the job. I brought some file folders with me, assuming he wanted to go over the books we had in the pipeline, the authors we were looking at for the future, and other items of business.

As we sat down to lunch, he said, "You're part of this group of men from Campus Crusade that is approaching the Orthodox Church to be received."

I said, "That's right."

He said, "Tell me about it."

So instead of talking books and business, we spent the time

at lunch talking about the ancient Orthodox Christian faith and why we Evangelicals were strongly drawn to it. Mike went on to become the president of Thomas Nelson and also a deacon in the Orthodox Church. Later, when Sam retired, Mike served as CEO and then as the chairman of the board for the company, leading Nelson to become what is now the largest Christian publishing company in the world. He is one of the most single-minded men I have ever met. He beautifully navigates the tension between business responsibilities and his relationship to Christ and his wife and five daughters. Mike has been one of my heroes, and I have counted it a privilege to call him a close friend.

CHAPTER 12

The Orthodox Study Bible

*"Don't you dare die, or this project
will never be completed."*

About a year after I had resigned from my publishing post at Thomas Nelson, was ordained to the priesthood, and had taken up my role as Director of Missions and Evangelism for the Antiochian Archdiocese, Sam Moore called me one day at my home in Santa Barbara, California. He said, "You know, I got to thinking: we've done a study Bible for every group under the sun here at Nelson. We have Catholic and Wesleyan study Bible versions, as well as others. But we have nothing for the Orthodox. Would you and your former Evangelical Protestant friends be willing to put together an Orthodox study Bible for us?"

I said, "Sam, from your Orthodox background, you know I can't answer that question by myself. I love the idea, but I'm going to need to get Metropolitan Philip's blessing in order for us to be able to undertake this."

He said, "I understand."

I approached the metropolitan with the project, and he was eager to give a green light to the creation of an editorial board and a group of workers to produce an Orthodox study Bible.

Sam and I were both well aware that though it was the Orthodox Church that gave us the Bible and protected it over the centuries, nonetheless many Orthodox Christians were not as schooled in the Scriptures as Evangelical Christians. We knew we had a challenge before us.

We put together a blue ribbon advisory board that consisted of leading Orthodox hierarchs, priests, and members of the laity. We also brought together a group of scholars who were equipped to do the notes and the commentary on the text. Very early in the project, we decided it would be safer to dip our big toe in the water and do only the New Testament and the Psalms, rather than the entire Bible. The Orthodox are committed to the Septuagint text of the Old Testament—the ancient Greek text used by Christ and the apostles and still in use in the Orthodox Church—but there was no modern Orthodox Christian translation of that text, and the task of producing one would be gargantuan.

Thomas Nelson owned the rights to the New King James Version, one of two translations that most American hierarchs preferred as a text appropriate for Orthodox Christians. The decision was made to produce *The Orthodox Study Bible, Volume One: New Testament and Psalms*. The team labored for years to put together the notes that would accompany the biblical text.

Shortly before the Bible went to print, Sam called again. "Father Peter, how many Bibles should we print?" he asked me.

I said, "Sam, you know as well as I do that Orthodox Christians have not set the world on fire in their zeal as Bible readers. So let me ask you: how many copies do you need to publish before you break even?"

Fr. Peter in 1991, during work on the OSB

He said, "Twenty-five thousand copies."

I gulped. I said, "Okay. If you produce twenty-five thousand of them, and we do a decent job of promotion, I'll promise you we will work to make sure that they sell."

There are so few things in life that turn out better than you ever dared dream, and this was one of them. We advertised the Bible through some Orthodox newspaper and magazine outlets and sent direct mailing pieces to the churches. We had made a specific decision that the cover of the Bible would be an icon of Jesus Christ and that a select group of four-color icons would be used throughout the text. This, we felt, would give Orthodox readers a sense of ownership of the Bible. They could say, "This is ours."

Two weeks before the publication date, those twenty-five thousand copies had sold out. Sam called again and announced he was rushing another twenty-five thousand into print. By the time those Bibles appeared in the market, that second printing had sold out.

The first year we sold a hundred thousand copies, and we couldn't keep them in print. Fast-forward to the early 1990s, when we began work on the complete version that included both the Old and New Testaments. At that point, we had sold nearly a half-million copies to a group of readers who were not known to be Bible students.

In those years after the New Testament and Psalms edition was published, the most thrilling thing for me would be to go into an Orthodox Christian home or parish and find dog-eared copies of the Bible: on coffee tables, on bedroom nightstands, and sometimes in the parish council rooms of churches that also doubled as a men's or women's Bible study room during the week.

When the decision was made and the blessing given to complete the project of doing the Old Testament portion of the Study Bible, which would include the translation of the Greek text into English, again the job before us was herculean. But this time so many of the people who were blessed by the New Testament and Psalms were willing to contribute financially. This enabled three of our Study Bible team members—Fr. Jack Sparks, Fr. Richard Ballew, and Paul Goetz—to devote a great deal of time to the project. In turn, they coordinated some ninety other scholars and clergy to do the translation and annotation work. Sam Moore himself donated a large amount to get us going.

It should have been the kind of project where those involved would meet in person frequently to compare notes, but the resources simply were not available to underwrite such a venture. Instead, we held *one* meeting at Antiochian Village in rural western Pennsylvania. In the meeting, we launched the project with about fifty of the contributors present. We outlined our project goals, editorial philosophy, and editorial guidelines.

We committed ourselves to a specific text of the Septuagint that is used to this day by the Orthodox Church of Greece. We also made a commitment to keep the language of both the translation and the notes simple enough to be understood by a high school graduate. This would not be Bible commentary by theologians to theologians, but commentary by theologians to the laity. We did receive a bit of criticism for this philosophy, but it has certainly proved to be valid: If we're going to bring Orthodoxy to America, our laity have got to be able to understand the faith well enough to discuss it with their non-Orthodox friends and family.

The preparation of the full Old and New Testaments of the Study Bible was probably the hardest thing most of us involved in leadership had ever done. During the waning years of the project, we lost two of the three key people: Fr. Jack Sparks began to deal with debilitating dementia, and our key lay leader, Paul Goetz, nearly died of sepsis, a total-body infection. He went into a coma, and the doctors did not expect him to live.

This meant the only full-time employee left was Fr. Richard Ballew. I remember saying to him, "Don't you dare die, or this project will never be completed." He was our Greek scholar who combed through everything, checking our team's translation against the Greek text. Fortunately there was a deacon in Sacramento, Dn. Polycarp Whitcomb, who was able to fill in for the work that Paul Goetz was doing, and I was asked to finish up the work Fr. Jack had begun.

During the time Paul Goetz was in a coma, nobody knew the password into his computer, in which all the text and notes of the Study Bible were kept. Of course, we immediately began falling behind in our editorial deadlines. Deacon Polycarp's wife Lisa was no tech person herself, but she decided to go over to Paul's home office to try to figure out the password. She said that she typed in every word she could think of, from "theosis" to "Theotokos" to "Orthodox" to "studybible," but with no luck. Paul's wife Anastasia wasn't able to help, since she knew little about computers and had no idea how to arrive at Paul's password.

Finally, Lisa looked up at the wall on Paul's office and saw a triangular banner for the University of Wisconsin, his alma mater. He was a die-hard Wisconsin fan and had also in his earlier years served in the state house as the youngest legislator in the history of Wisconsin. Lisa typed in "Wisconsin," and that didn't work. Then she typed in "Badgers," the UW mascot, and bingo! The whole computer lit up. So, through the grace of God, we had only a two-week delay, and we were able to again access the records that Paul Goetz had kept so carefully in the computer.

I once said to Bob Sanford, an Orthodox priest who was also Vice President of Bibles at Thomas Nelson, "I think the devil has thrown every trick in his book at us in making sure this project wouldn't come to light."

He said, "Everybody I've ever worked with who misses a publishing deadline says the same thing, but in your case, I think you're right!"

So "through many dangers, toils, and snares" we were finally able to present a final manuscript to Thomas Nelson for *The Orthodox Study Bible, Old and New Testaments*. The finished product has been widely accepted in Orthodox Christian communities, not only in the English-speaking world but internationally, as well. We were told that of all the Orthodox books ever published in English, this one leads the pack for sales and distribution. Beyond those numbers, we are thrilled to know that Orthodox Christians are using the Bible for personal study, as an aid to teaching Orthodox Bible studies (which until its publication rarely existed), and as an aid to clergy. Priests have often told us, "The Study Bible absolutely saved the day for me last Sunday!" We thank God not only that it's being sold but more importantly that it's being used.

People have asked me, "What do you think will be your greatest legacy as converts to the Church?" I could mention the number of churches that have been founded through converts, or I could mention the reawakening to missions and evangelism that has occurred in the modern Orthodox Church. But I think when all is said and done, perhaps the greatest contribution we've been blessed to make will be the publication and reception of *The Orthodox Study Bible* in the English-speaking world.

CHAPTER 13

The Evangelicals
and the Orthodox

"What is it about us that you don't like?"

Sir, are we saved by faith or by works?" The scene was in suburban Milwaukee, Wisconsin, at St. Nicholas Orthodox Church,
and the inquisitor was a visitor from one of the local Evangelical Bible churches. We were at coffee hour doing a question-and-
answer session after my homily earlier that morning. I could tell
by looking at him that he had that "gotcha" look in his eyes.

My answer was, "Neither!" Not only his face went blank, but
also the faces of most of the hundred or so people present for coffee hour.

"Think about it," I said to him. "Let's start with works. Jesus
said, 'Be ye perfect as My Father in heaven is perfect.' So obviously, if we're saved by works, we've got to be absolutely perfect in
our works. Does anybody here make the cut?" No hands went up.
"That isn't to minimize the importance of doing works that glo-
rify God, but it does underscore that, because we're fallen people,
there's no way works alone can save us.

"Now let's switch over to faith. Anybody here have perfect faith?" Again, no hands went up. "Is faith important to us and our salvation? Absolutely. But none of us is going to check into heaven with a hundred percent on our final exam, whether the subject is faith or works. So again we're brought back to St. Paul in the Book of Romans, that 'all have sinned and fall short of the glory of God' (Rom. 3:23).

"The fact is," I continued, "if we're going to be saved, it'll have to be by the mercy of God, because it's God's mercy that brings us from where we are to where we need to be." Then I used a story my fellow priest Fr. Alexander Veronis had told years earlier. It's fiction, of course, and it's neither biblical nor patristic, but it does make the point.

An Orthodox man died and went up before the pearly gates of heaven to meet St. Peter. Saint Peter said to him, "It's going to take one hundred points to get you in here."

The man replied, "I don't recall reading anything like that, either in the Scripture or in the patristic writings of the Church." But then he thought, *Who am I to argue with St. Peter?*

Saint Peter said, "Tell me some of the things you did to bring glory to God while you were on earth."

The man thought for a time and then said, "Well, for two years I taught Sunday school for our high school kids."

"Very well," St. Peter said. "That'll be ten points."

"Also, for many years, I sang in the choir."

"Okay, that'll be fifteen points."

"I also served by helping Father in the altar during the Divine Liturgy."

"Fine. That's another ten points."

"Oh, and I forgot. I served two terms on the parish council."

Saint Peter said, "That's minus fifteen points."

The guy threw his hands up in despair and said to St. Peter, "It's going to take the mercy of God to get me in here!"

Then St. Peter said, "And that will be one hundred points."

The fact is, none of us, either through our works or through our faith, are ever going to come up spotless or in any way able to merit our salvation. In the end, it's got to be the mercy of God that qualifies us.

Several years ago at a well-known Christian school, a faculty member expressed concern about Orthodox faculty and staff members. Those Orthodox Christians were asked to explain their beliefs, and then the administration of the school would decide whether or not the Orthodox employees passed muster theologically and could be allowed to continue in their positions.

One of the Orthodox Christian employees phoned me to get my advice. "Here's what I would suggest you do," I said. "As you walk into the president's office, remember that both he and you are going to be very uncomfortable. Nobody likes a showdown. So before the meeting begins, ask if you can be allowed to say a few words."

He said, "Okay, what do I say?"

I said, "Here's what I would say if I were you: 'I just want you brothers to understand that as an Orthodox Christian, I believe in the Holy Trinity. I believe in the full deity and the full humanity of Jesus Christ. I believe that we're saved by faith. I believe in the work of Christ.' And then quote from the Creed: 'The cross, the tomb, the resurrection from the dead, the ascension into heaven, the seating at the right hand of the Father, and the second and glorious coming.'

"Also," I continued, "you can say, 'As I'm sure you believe, I believe that homosexual acts are sinful, and that to take the life of an unborn baby is tantamount to murder. I also believe in the inspiration and the authority of the Scriptures. So perhaps you can explain, what is it about us that you don't like?'"

He called me back later and said that ended the meeting.

Usually, most of what Evangelicals don't like about Orthodox is the externals. They don't like the clerical collars. They don't like the vestments. They don't like the icons. They don't like the large three-bar crosses. They may not like the fact that we chant the Scriptures when we read them as opposed to simply saying them. They don't like prolonged periods of fasting, though this has always been a Church practice from the very beginning.

Yet when it comes right down to it, the Orthodox and the Evangelicals share way more in common than they differ on. A great challenge of our time is that we learn how to get along with and understand one another.

Right before I became Orthodox, I was asked to speak to a large Orthodox gathering at Ss. Peter and Paul Orthodox Church in Glenview, Illinois, pastored by Fr. George Scoulas, a marvelous man of God and Christ-centered priest. Also present that night was his bishop, which I admit made me a little bit nervous. My job was to tell our story and why it was that we were seeking to come into the Orthodox Church.

As was my usual custom, before the meeting was over I opened it up to questions. One of the first questions asked was about Orthodox Christian unity and the perceived need for it across jurisdictional lines. I answered as best I could and found myself challenged from the floor by the bishop. Thankfully, no rancor proceeded from that disagreement, and we went on with the meeting. The bishop and I have become good friends since then, although we still hold different opinions about Orthodox unity in the United States.

The next day, in my position as book editor at Thomas Nelson, I had lunch with a large and influential Protestant pastor in Chicago. He requested we eat at a nearby restaurant that was known for its outstanding Greek cuisine. Despite the fact that I was wearing my business suit and tie, our waitress recognized me and asked somewhat haltingly, "Weren't you the priest who spoke at our church last night out in Glenview?"

I said, "Yes."

She said, "I just enjoyed so much your presentation and wanted to say thank you."

In the meantime, the pastor I was having lunch with asked her a question. "Ma'am, do you mind if I ask, how is it that we as Christians are saved?"

The waitress responded, "By doing the best we can."

If I could have, I would have slid under the table. Yet if she as a Greek Orthodox Christian had had a chance to answer follow-up questions, she probably would have said, "Well, in the last analysis, it's got to be by the grace of God." It was so difficult to know how to explain the Orthodox Christian understanding of salvation to this pastor with all his preconceived Protestant ideas. I didn't believe that's how we're saved, and I knew that at the end of the day, she didn't believe that's how we're saved.

My plea to Protestants has always been, "Let's learn to listen to each other." Instead of rejecting each other out of hand, let's work to at least gain some understanding and bring the mercy of God into our conversations. I've said so often that if it weren't for Evangelical Christians, I don't think I'd be a Christian of any stripe today.

I view our Evangelical brethren in much the same way as St. Paul approached his Jewish brethren. His desire was to bring his brothers and sisters into the fullness of the faith that was once for all revealed to the saints by our Incarnate God, the Lord Jesus Christ, and he spent his entire life on that mission. Even though he was specifically the apostle to the Gentiles, nonetheless, in Romans 9, 10, and 11, we discover that St. Paul's heart's desire and cry for Israel is that they might become part of this new and everlasting covenant.

In the same way, my desire for our Evangelical brethren is that they would at least take the time to understand why it is that so many Evangelicals are returning to the ancient faith and practice of the Orthodox Church. I have never viewed my Protestant brethren with condemnation or judgment.

People have sometimes asked me if I believe I was a participant in salvation back in my Evangelical days. I always say, "Absolutely yes." I loved Christ, I loved His people, and I loved His Scriptures. Yet the deeper we went into our faith, the more we discovered the fullness of the faith of the early Church and how it had survived throughout the centuries of the Church through the Orthodox.

A short time after I was ordained, I returned to the campus of Dallas Seminary, this time in my clerical garb. The secretary of one of the administrative leaders of the seminary asked me a question when I entered her office.

She said, "Sir, are you saved?"

I said to her, "Constantly."

She didn't know what to do with the answer. Devout Christians outside of the Orthodox Christian Church often really want to know: Are the Orthodox really Christian? I think our challenge is to converse freely with one another to determine what it is that each community believes and why they believe it.

Years ago when I was on the staff at Campus Crusade, two of our key students at Michigan State University were the children of Mr. and Mrs. Ed Cole. Ed was the president of General Motors, and one night his daughter Marti asked us to speak to a group of her high school friends in their home. It was my one chance to meet a man who was a visionary and automotive industry heavyweight.

Ed walked down the stairs into his finished basement, and I decided to follow him. I said, "Do you mind if I ask you one question?" I was probably twenty-five, and he was in his mid-fifties.

He said, "Go ahead. What is it?"

I said, "Of all the men who have been privileged to be college graduates and graduates of GMI (General Motors Institute outside of Detroit), and then among the thousands and thousands of employees of General Motors, why is it that you rose to the top?"

He paused for a moment and said, "I love problems."

As one who doesn't love problems, I've never forgotten his response. But I think the greatest challenge in the Christendom of our day, especially in North America, is for the Orthodox and the Evangelicals, who hold so many things in common, to learn to come together to dialogue without rancor. We need to share why we believe as we do. Any Orthodox Christian worth his salt ought to admire the zeal and the love for Christ and the Bible of the average Evangelical. And any Evangelical with a working knowledge of church history has to acknowledge that the worship of the Church after the New Testament era was liturgical, sacramental, and hierarchical.

CHAPTER 14

Mentors

*"Is there not still someone left . . . to whom I may
show the mercy of God?"*

One of the most moving chapters in the Old Testament is
2 Samuel 9 (in the Septuagint, 2 Kingdoms). David has
been enthroned as king over all Israel. He has entered into a covenant with God of tremendous import for his people. As chapter 9 opens, he's evidently wistful over friendships of his past,
because the text reads, "Now David said, 'Is there anyone still left
of the house of Saul, so that I may show him mercy for Jonathan's
sake?'" (2 Sam. 9:1).

Thinking back to David's childhood, we remember that he and
Jonathan, the son of Saul, were the best of friends. Their friendship was an icon of true brotherhood between two men. At this
point in David's life, he is drawn to honor his friendship with
Jonathan by seeking out one of his descendants to whom he could
show mercy.

*And there was a servant of the house of Saul whose
name was Ziba, and they called him to David. And
the king said to him, "Are you Ziba?" And he said, "I*

am your servant!" Then the king said, "Is there not still someone left in the house of Saul, to whom I may show the mercy of God?" (2 Sam. 9:2–3)

And it turns out, there was.

And Ziba said to the king, "There is still a son of Jonathan who is wounded in his feet." So the king said to him, "Where is he?" And Ziba said to the king, "See, he is in the house of Machir the son of Ammiel, in Lo Debar." (2 Sam. 9:3–4)

From our linguistic studies, we know that the literal meaning of Lo Debar is "wasteland." In other words, the son of David's best friend is basically in a no-man's-land situation. The son's name was Mephibosheth. Second Samuel 9:6 opens this way:

When Mephibosheth the son of Jonathan, the son of Saul, had come to King David, he fell on his face and prostrated before him. Then David said, "Mephibosheth?" And he answered, "Here is your servant!" So David said to him, "Do not fear, for I will surely show mercy for the sake of Jonathan your father. I will restore to you all the land of Saul your grandfather, and you shall always eat bread at my table." Then Mephibosheth bowed and said, "Who am I, your servant, that you should look upon a dead dog like me?" (2 Sam. 9:6–8)

I guess that's a question many of us ask as we are confronted with the mercy of God: "Why me? What on earth have I done to deserve this?" Of course He answers, "Nothing." Mercy is not something we earn. Whether it's from the Lord Himself or from another human being, it always comes to us as a gift—or it really isn't mercy.

So David moves this crippled young man into his house, and every night he can hear the clump-clump of these two lame feet across the floor to take his place at the king's table. Of course, this is also an incredible picture of the Holy Eucharist, as we who are sinners and fallen out of the state in which God created us into sin, lame though we may be, still by His mercy find a way to His holy table to feast with the King of kings.

This story from the Old Testament beautifully demonstrates God's compassion for mankind and King David's compassion toward the son of his dearest childhood friend, Jonathan.

Thinking back over our own journey to the Orthodox Church, which culminated in our reception under the Patriarch of Antioch by the hands of His Eminence Metropolitan Philip, the primate of the Antiochian Archdiocese here in North America, many names come to mind of those who brought God's mercy to us.

The first Orthodox bishop I ever met was Dmitri, who went on to be Bishop and then Archbishop of Dallas and the South for the Orthodox Church in America (OCA). Vladyka Dmitri was on a visitation trip to the West Coast and had asked to meet with our group of Evangelicals in Santa Barbara, California, who were studying the Orthodox faith. Through this encounter, which remains vividly in my memory, we learned to address an Orthodox bishop as "Your Grace." When I met him and began to get to know him, I thought to myself, "What an appropriate title for this man!" He was one of the most gracious men I had ever met.

Carrying all the dignity of a bishop of the Church, he

nonetheless was anything but distant; instead, he was very warm and centered in his Lord and Master, Jesus Christ. We were amazed to learn that, like so many of us, he had been brought up in an Evangelical Protestant setting, the child of devout Southern Baptist parents.

His story was simply this: At age fifteen, the young Robert Royster and his sister (given the Orthodox names Dmitri and Dimitra at conversion) had found their way to a small Greek Orthodox church on the south side of Dallas, where they attended the Divine Liturgy on a Sunday morning. Everything was in Greek, and they understood very little of what was taking place, but both siblings realized this was unlike anything they had ever experienced as Christians. Within a short while they were received into the Church. Bishop Dmitri told us he remembered his mother asking them, did the Orthodox Church believe in Jesus Christ as Savior and Lord? To which Dmitri and Dimitra replied, "Yes." At which point she said, "Then you have my blessing to go."

Our fledgling Orthodox community in Santa Barbara received great comfort from his story; Bishop Dmitri seemed to understand us in a deeper way than any Orthodox person we had met thus far, and, of course, his story was similar to what would become our story.

On a subsequent trip to Dallas, I had the joy of meeting Bishop Dmitri's right-hand man, Fr. Thomas Green, a former Episcopalian priest who had become Orthodox. While sitting in the living room with Fr. Thomas and his dog, I said, "What's your dog's name?"

"Moreover," replied Fr. Thomas.

I said, "'Moreover'? Where did you get that name?" As I looked at him, I knew it was a question he wanted me to ask. He said, "Moreover the dog came and licked his wounds" (Luke 16:21).

Father Thomas was as genial a man as there is, and as several more in our community got to know him, we discovered that he was dean of the cathedral and of the area priests. Somehow we came up with the nickname for this very gentle man, "Mean Dean Green," and that's how we knew him and referred to him up until the time of his death some years later.

Another hero to those of us seeking the Orthodox path was the incomparable Fr. Alexander Schmemann. So many people told us, "If you're ever in New York, give him a call and meet him!" Sometime in the late 1970s, I was in New York on publishing business, and while in the city, I called Fr. Alexander on the phone. He said, "I'll meet you under the clock at Grand Central Station." Later someone told me this was one of his favorite places to meet people, since he enjoyed having lunch at a little café there in the terminal.

As we visited, it became apparent to me with even greater clarity that the Orthodox Christian path isn't learned and mastered overnight. Here I was in my early forties, quite well educated in things biblical and theological, and yet I felt I had never been with someone so far ahead of me, biblically and theologically, in my entire life. At times he spoke in categories I knew nothing about. Yet I could also sense that here was a man who had a heartfelt and steadfast love for Christ and for His Church.

On later occasions, our parish invited him to come to Santa Barbara to speak to a council of bishops that our group, the Evangelical Orthodox Church, had formed in 1979. We were amazed at his depth and knowledge of historic Christianity.

In addition to the guidance of Fr. Schmemann, the input from his successor at St. Vladimir's Seminary, Fr. John Meyendorff, was of great help to us as well. In the early 1980s, Fr. John and I were invited to be co-speakers at a large seminar at St. Thomas College, a Roman Catholic school in St. Paul, Minnesota. I welcomed the invitation because it gave me an opportunity to work side by side with Fr. John while also visiting with my Minneapolis family.

At the end of one of his presentations, someone asked him a question, *the* question. "Do you think the Evangelical Orthodox will find their way into the canonical Orthodox Church?"

Father John Meyendorff answered, "My fear is not that they will not come; my fear is that we might not receive them." I can still remember the blood draining out of my head as I processed this statement, wondering, *What on earth does he mean by this?* Later I was to learn more of the complexities of Orthodox jurisdictions and governance.

The background and life story of our friend and mentor Bishop Maximos of Pittsburgh (Greek Orthodox Archdiocese) were completely different from those of Fr. John, Fr. Alexander, or Bishop Dmitri. Bishop Maximos was born into the Orthodox Church in a small village in Greece and later immigrated to America. Yet like Bishop Dmitri, he was a gifted theologian and pastor who understood us in a way few others did. At my first visit to his home and diocesan headquarters on Ellsworth Avenue in Pittsburgh, I was welcomed with warm hospitality.

Bishop Maximos seemed to recognize that we were sincere pilgrims and sojourners; a short time later he invited me to come back to Pittsburgh and speak to the Orthodox Christian Fellowship of Greater Pittsburgh (OCF). The chapters of OCF all consisted of Orthodox students from schools like Duquesne, the University of Pittsburgh, and Carnegie Mellon. For this occasion there was a dinner at Duranti's Restaurant (Mrs. Duranti was Greek Orthodox), and perhaps two hundred Orthodox college kids were present, along with many of the Pittsburgh clergy.

I spoke to them out of my own experience, telling them how I had committed my life to Jesus Christ as a junior at the University of Minnesota. My closing remarks referred to Revelation 3:14–21, which is the story of the lukewarm Laodicean Christians, whom Jesus exhorted to follow Him with greater zeal. It was one of those nights when the Holy Spirit seemed to descend upon a gathering. I'll never forget one young man; as he walked out of the room that night he said, "Father, you gave me the kick in the butt that I needed." Two decades later, I met him again at an Orthodox banquet in Pittsburgh, and we still remembered each other and that scene very vividly.

Two of the priests in the diocese Bishop Maximos oversaw were Fr. Alexander Veronis, pastor of Annunciation Church in Lancaster, Pennsylvania, and Fr. John Chakos, the pastor of Holy Cross Greek Orthodox Church in Pittsburgh. Both of these men had incredible hearts for missions and evangelism, and we had an instant and enduring connection.

Another priest who showed us great mercy in our early days in the Orthodox faith was Fr. Thomas Hopko, later the dean of St. Vladimir's Seminary. The son-in-law of Fr. Alexander Schmemann, Fr. Tom had the demeanor of a blunt New Yorker. He was always fully honest with anyone he spoke with, and we had to get used to his style. Nonetheless, he was an important mentor as well, since he stretched us in the places where we needed to be challenged and encouraged us to forsake all to follow Christ within His holy, catholic, and apostolic Church.

On Fr. Tom's final visit with us in Santa Barbara, about a year before we were received by the hands of Metropolitan Philip into the Church, he and I sat together for our parish's rendition of the Divine Liturgy, which we had essentially learned out of the service books. I was so proud of the way Fr. Richard Ballew conducted the service, assisted by a couple of his deacons. At the benediction, I turned to Fr. Tom and said, "Well, what do you think?"

He said, "I only counted seventy-two errors."

"You've got to be kidding."

"Honestly, most of them were very minor."

"What was the worst one?"

He said, "Your deacon censed the church backwards."

It was at this point we realized that to be Orthodox, people must have spiritual directors, just as when playing football, team members need more than a playbook—they need a coach. Father Tom's visit was a critical turning point for us. We realized in a new way that Orthodox Christianity isn't an individual sport, but rather a team effort. And the coaches aren't just the spiritual guides on site, but those men and women who have gone on before us to their rest over the past two-thousand–year history of the Church.

As I've alluded to before in my book *Becoming Orthodox*, one of our great frustrations in these years would be that we would ultimately have to respond to an invitation to enter the Church through one of the various jurisdictions of Orthodoxy in America. Our fear was not so much that we would make a false choice, but that when we did choose, it would cancel out the incredible friendships we had made over the fifteen years or so of our journey with people from all the Orthodox jurisdictions.

With deep gratitude, we realized later that this fear was unfounded. To this day, I count all of these gentlemen and many others too numerous to mention as dear friends whose friendship, if anything, grew stronger after we entered the Church. Bishop Maximos is forever a friend and brother in Christ whom I will love into eternity. Bishop Dmitri, later Archbishop Dmitri, is now of blessed memory, but I still count on him as a present and forever friend.

One of the great thrills of my life was that on the twenty-fifth anniversary of his elevation to the episcopacy, Bishop Dmitri could have invited anybody in the Orthodox world to come and speak at the banquet that honored him, but for whatever reason he chose me. Even though we didn't enter the Church through the door of his jurisdiction, the OCA, that didn't make a bit of difference when I spoke at the anniversary.

On the Saturday afternoon before the banquet, Bishop Dmitri invited me to speak with his diocesan clergy who had come to honor him. I was able to talk about the work I was doing in heading up the missions and evangelism effort for the Antiochian Archdiocese and recounted the ways in which the bishop and I both related to Protestant pastors who had come to one of us asking to be received along with some of their people. Additionally, I described the strategies we would use in choosing a town with a significant population base in America in which there was no

Orthodox church of any jurisdiction; we would then make contact and build relationships with Orthodox and non-Orthodox Christians who were open to becoming part of the local Church.

Missionary efforts in the Western world are relatively new for the Orthodox Christian Church. Neither the Orthodox hierarchs nor any in our group of spiritual seekers really knew what to do; the entrance of two thousand apple-pie American, Billy Graham–type Christians as a body into the Orthodox Church here in America had simply never happened before. The jurisdictional bodies we approached within Orthodoxy were confused and divided about how to handle our unusual movement, as were we. But many cradle Orthodox along the way were incredibly gracious and became our mentors and guides.

My greatest mentor and hero was His Eminence Metropolitan Philip of the Antiochian Archdiocese. He put his bishopric on the line for us, and after much study and deliberation, he opened the doors to receive us into the fold of the Antiochian Archdiocese of North America. Until my dying day and beyond, there will not be a day when I do not thank the Lord for Sayidna Philip: for his courage and for his boldness in being willing to take a step which, at that point, few if any others were willing to take. To him I am eternally grateful.

CHAPTER 15

Learning the Ropes

*"Sometimes they make you king first,
and then you learn how."*

My fellow Antiochian priest and longtime friend Fr. Jon Braun tells the story of when he was in seminary in Chicago and was known as the campus prankster. One day the dean of students called him in and said, "Jon, what you've got to learn is that in any given situation there are parameters. And here at North Park"— he put his hands out parallel to each other on his desk—"the parameters are here to here. Now," he said, raising one hand and putting it down, raising the other hand and putting it down, "I can't always tell you where here and here is, but as a student here, you've got to operate inside the parameters of here and here."

Father Jon later said this brief conversation changed his life. He realized that in every new situation he would encounter, he would be entering into an established tradition that, like it or not, had boundaries and expectations that needed to be navigated and understood.

Growing up Lutheran, I knew how to navigate the Lutheran

Church. I knew what was expected of me as a young person, what the services were like, and how we were expected to behave in those services. I knew how to behave in Sunday school, and I knew what to eat at the smorgasbord served in the parish hall after church. People say, "I'm comfortable in my own skin," and I was comfortable in my own surroundings.

Going off to college, I learned about new parameters in the classroom and in the fraternity—some of which I didn't even agree with—but you still had to stay between here and here. In seminary and in Campus Crusade, I learned my way around the Evangelical world. There were things that were expected. You could certainly be creative, but somewhere or other, there were boundaries you did not pass over.

This is basically true in every culture I've ever been in. Even in Memphis, where I worked with the drug kids and the Satan-worshiping kids, I found strong parameters in that culture. You never crossed the Big Guy, and you also paid your bills if you were doing drugs on credit. The alternative was awful.

Similarly, when a group of Western Christians enters the Orthodox Church, there are parameters that are learned through experience. In Orthodox worship, physically able people stand. They don't sit, and for sure they don't kick back. Orthodox hymns are sung as prayers, and hymns are never self-focused. Instead, they're all about the Father, the Son, and the Holy Spirit, and our love and adoration toward that one, true God.

Being a Christian in an Orthodox setting is not a request-and-demand relationship. Earth never tells heaven what to do. There's no sense of "I name it and I claim it, and God is bound to fulfill it," but rather that we come to Him as the Scriptures teach, with great humility, begging Him for His mercy rather than demanding it.

Shortly after we resigned from working for the Campus Crusade staff, I began to have a recurring dream. In an ancient part of a European city, I would see an old church constructed of very dark stone, similar to edifices built many centuries ago in Trier, Germany, where all the buildings are nearly black with age.

In my dream, I would become the pastor of this old stone church, with the mandate to bring new life to the venerable community through the preaching of the Gospel. I didn't have the dream just a few nights, but many times over in a span of maybe five years.

Of course the dream never literally came true; I never did become pastor of an old church in the heart of a European city. But figuratively, it depicted our journey. Ultimately our group of seekers would bring thousands of people into the oldest Church in Christendom and by God's mercy also breathe new enthusiasm and life into an ancient and honorable faith. I use the word "enthusiasm" advisedly, because its root word is *entheos* (ἔνθεος), which in the Greek literally means "in God." Enthusiasm is the result of being in God. It's something you don't manufacture; it is a gift that He gives.

Saint Paul warns in the Book of Colossians about taking a stand based on dreams and visions, and I have heeded that warning. The only stock I put in that dream is that it served rather as an ancillary witness to the fact that part of our purpose together in life was to rediscover the ancient Church and the ancient Christian faith, and by God's mercy to become part of it.

On our twenty-fifth wedding anniversary, Marilyn and I had

an interesting experience that taught us the importance of learning the ropes in new situations. I was still employed by Thomas Nelson. The company owned an executive apartment on 34th and Lexington in New York City, a beautiful eighteenth-floor suite with a balcony that overlooked the Empire State Building. With six kids and a tight budget, we still found New York hotels pretty much out of reach, so I called Sam Moore and asked if it would be possible for us to use the apartment to celebrate our twenty-fifth wedding anniversary. He kindly obliged.

We flew to New York on a Thursday heading into Memorial Day weekend and took a cab to the apartment. On Friday morning, I telephoned a theater on Broadway where Yul Brynner was in his closing months of playing in *The King and I* opposite Mary Beth Peil. I said, "I'd like a couple seats for the matinee tomorrow."

The man said, "Sir, you are out of your mind."

"What do you mean?"

"This stuff has been sold out for months. The last performance will be sometime in August or September. There are absolutely no seats available for anything."

I said, "Forgive me. I'm from California. I know nothing about New York theater."

"There are just simply no seats." Then he paused for a second and said, "Wait a minute! Two seats just popped up in the orchestra section for tomorrow afternoon."

I said, "Grab 'em."

And for fifty bucks a seat, we got to see Yul Brynner in one of his final performances as the king of Siam from the fourth row back from the stage. We'd seen the movie, but we'd never seen the play. Despite the fact that Marilyn had come down with some kind of bug and was not feeling well, we loved every moment of the performance.

The closing scene of *The King and I* occurs outside the opaque curtain, where the nanny is speaking with the young heir to the throne. In the background, through a see-through curtain, the deceased king is lying on a bier, and the conversation goes something like this.

The little boy says, "But he never taught me how to be king."

And the nanny says, "Sometimes first they make you king, and then you learn how."

It was a eureka moment for us. By now we knew the basics of the Orthodox faith pretty well, but we didn't know the ropes. How would we navigate within this new culture and this new Church? That one line gave us both great hope that the Lord would be present with us, merciful as always, to give us the ability to learn the Orthodox culture from within. It simply cannot be learned from the outside, so we were going to find out what the parameters were, between here and here, and then we would begin to understand how to live within those parameters.

There are moments that are funny now that weren't when they first happened. One of those was right before we were brought into the Church. Marilyn and I were invited to come to New York for the twentieth-anniversary celebration of the episcopacy of Metropolitan Philip. We were so heartened by the service at St. Nicholas Cathedral on Sunday morning because we discovered that not only did we have the opportunity to learn the centuries-old Orthodox hymns, but also during the time of Communion and the veneration of the cross at the end of the service we sang several of our favorite Christmas carols, such as "Silent Night" and "O Come, All Ye Faithful" (a hymn, by the way, with origins in the ancient Church).

Sunday evening was the reception and banquet honoring the metropolitan. The priest who drove us to the banquet that night, Fr. Antony Gabriel of Montreal, later became a good friend. When we arrived at the banquet facility, we were ushered into the reception area, which was filled with bishops and prominent clergy. We were amazed that we were even included in this august assembly.

Father John Meyendorff, then the dean at St. Vladimir's Seminary, asked Marilyn if she had met Archbishop Iakovos, the head of the Greek Orthodox Archdiocese of North and South America. Though I had met him, Marilyn had not, and so he graciously said, "Come, let me introduce you to him." Marilyn greeted the archbishop with a kiss on the hand and said, "Your Grace, it's very good to meet you."

It was only an hour or so later as the guests at the head table were being introduced that she realized he was introduced as His Eminence Archbishop Iakovos rather than His Grace. Thus, the rest of the banquet was a long period of suffering for my dear and beloved wife.

Later, we learned that Archbishop Iakovos was a stickler for protocol!

I was with Archbishop Iakovos at a reception at his home just a few weeks before he died. The rest of our group was in another room getting refreshments, and he—by now an elderly gentleman confined to a chair—was waiting for someone else to bring him tea. One should never leave the bishop, or in this case the archbishop, sitting alone, so when others left the room, I pulled a chair up beside him to keep him company.

I said to him, "I've got something to thank you for."

"What is that?" he asked.

"Do you remember back in 1986, when it was Metropolitan Philip's twentieth anniversary in the episcopacy and we celebrated the Divine Liturgy in the cathedral in Brooklyn and then the banquet that evening on Staten Island?"

"Yes."

"Do you remember when Fr. John Meyendorff introduced my wife to you and she called you 'Your Grace'?"

And he said, "Yes."

"I'm here to thank you for not correcting her on the spot."

His reaction was a warm smile, and that's my last memory of him.

There is an Orthodox culture. It really does take a while to learn it, but just as with any body of people you'll ever be in, the Lord helps new members to navigate and learn the ropes. And gracious Orthodox Christians and mentors help too.

In 1979, our group of seeker parishes that had been on the long journey to the historic Church started the St. Athanasius Academy in Santa Barbara, California. By this time we were calling our group the Evangelical Orthodox Church, the story of which is told in my book *Becoming Orthodox*. Providentially, as our group was migrating west, Thomas Nelson also decided they wanted a West Coast presence and so allowed me to continue my editorial position from our new location. Once again, our family of eight packed our bags and relocated to Santa Barbara to our last family home. One by one, our "bears" began to move on to college, marriage, and new lives of their own.

In 1987 I was ordained to the holy priesthood and then continued my ministry to students and seekers from within the Orthodox Church. Many of my fellow Evangelical Orthodox ministers and parishioners joined the Church during this time. Our long journey was over; we had come home.

CHAPTER 16

For This Child I Prayed

"Father, do you believe in miracles?"

A few months after I was ordained to the priesthood, I was invited to offer a weekend retreat at a Greek Orthodox church in Columbus, Ohio. The bishop of the diocese was none other than my friend Bishop Maximos of Pittsburgh, and he had encouraged his clergy to invite new converts to the Church to come and tell our stories.

After the Divine Liturgy that Sunday morning, a group of married couples invited me out to lunch at the Old Spaghetti Factory in Columbus, and then one couple volunteered to escort me to the airport for an afternoon flight. After lunch, one by one the couples said good-bye and left. The couple that was providing my transportation was sitting across the table. I could tell especially that she wanted to talk.

She began the conversation by asking, "Father, do you believe in miracles?"

I said, "Yes."

"I wonder if you'd pray for my husband and me. We've been married for years, and we've tried everything we know to have children. So far we have not succeeded. Would you pray for us right now and ask God that if it's His will, we be given children?"

As a new priest, I wasn't familiar with the prayers of the Church and hadn't memorized the prayers of healing. I didn't have my service book with me, since it was packed in my suitcase, and I didn't have any holy oil to anoint them. So I simply reached across the table, laid my hands on each of their heads, and prayed a prayer of healing as best I could reconstruct it. I ended by making the sign of the cross on each of their foreheads. We stood up and exchanged hugs, and they loaded me in their car to take me to the airport.

About three months later, I got a card in the mail with a handwritten address, postmarked Columbus, Ohio. The wife was writing to tell me she was pregnant. Five or six months later, I received a birth announcement. I didn't stay in touch with this couple but was told by some mutual friends that she went on to have a second child and was so grateful to God for His mercy in granting them a family.

Fast-forward a year to 1991, when I was in Grand Rapids, Michigan, at the home of a couple who have become dear friends, Rob and Beth. They also had been married fifteen or sixteen years and had never been able to have children. This was the year the University of Michigan's team of five freshman players went on to win the NCAA basketball tournament. Beth had gone to bed, and Rob and I were sitting up in the den, watching the game. It was a Saturday night around eleven o'clock. As we watched the second half (Michigan won), Rob told me how he and Beth had wanted so badly to have a family and had gone to fertility clinics and specialists, yet hadn't been able to have a child.

I told him about the couple in Columbus and said, "Have you ever asked your priest to anoint you and pray the prayer of healing over you?"

He said, "It's amazing: as strongly Orthodox as we are, we never have."

"Well, tomorrow after church, why don't we gather, you two and I and your priest, and we'll anoint you and pray the healing prayers and ask God to give you children."

"You know, we've got a whole houseful of people coming over right after church on Sunday, and I know Beth will have to get home and prepare the food."

"Okay, then I'll ask Father for a small vial of oil, and we'll pray those prayers privately in your home."

Remembering back to that Sunday afternoon in Columbus, I was sure not to pack my stole and to keep my book of prayers with me. Sometime before the meal, I asked Beth if she could spare five minutes to go up into their room; I would read one of the healing Gospels and pray a couple of the prayers, asking that God heal whatever was keeping them from having children.

Again, three or four months passed, and I got a note in the mail, this time postmarked Grand Rapids. Beth was writing to explain that she had become pregnant. Another couple of months went by, and the next note simply said, "It's triplets!"

Since then, every Christmas Marilyn and I receive their holiday letter, and from the first Christmas of those kids' lives on to the present, we've watched them grow up, long-distance, through the gift of photography. I've still got many of those cards and pictures, and the triplets are college kids and wonderful Christians. (They are a girl and two boys.)

For whatever reason, at some point the Lord seemed to give me the gift of praying for barren couples. There are a couple of sets of twins around the country that I've prayed for. My own daughter and her husband were able to have two children after a struggle to conceive, and a number of couples we know have birthed one or two children after receiving the prayers of healing and the anointing of oil.

People say, "What's it like?" I need to say there's absolutely no rush, no fireworks, no warm feeling in my hands. I'm not against any of that, but for me it is an act of obedience to take God at His word and "let your requests be made known to God; and the peace of God, which surpasses all understanding, will guard your hearts and minds through Christ Jesus" (Phil. 4:6–7). It's one of the few verses in the Bible that doesn't promise the answer of "yes," but it does promise the gift of peace.

Certainly, not every couple I've prayed for has conceived, but an incredible number of them have, and I feel I know less about the miracles of God now than I did when I started out. It is simply His mercy. "I will have mercy on whom I will have mercy." It's a gift I love to employ, because it's totally out of my hands and yet, for me as a dad who loves his kids more than life itself, it's a marvelous way to help people experience the warmth of family that Marilyn and I have been so blessed to know.

CHAPTER 17

Romanian Journey

"May heaven consume you."

Over Labor Day, 1991, a spark was ignited at our annual Missions and Evangelism Conference. In God's providence, it developed into one of the most rewarding and fulfilling assignments I have ever been involved with as an Orthodox priest and evangelist.

During the course of our four-day weekend, Fr. Dan Suciu (letter in appendix), the dean of the Romanian Orthodox Cathedral in Regina, Saskatchewan, Canada, shared a plan with me that he believed God had been laying on his heart throughout the conference. "What would be the possibility," he asked, "of forming an outreach team composed of American and Romanian Orthodox priests that would embark on an evangelistic preaching tour to Romania?"

Father Dan went on to explain that since the fall of communism, Romania has been literally besieged by American missionaries. The Charismatics, the Pentecostals, Non-Trinitarian Pentecostals, the Baptists, and the cults had been hard at work "converting the Orthodox." For the most part, even the mainline Christians hadn't drawn any distinctions between trying to convert pagans to Christianity and trying to persuade lifelong Orthodox people to "become Christians." Great confusion was resulting.

"Just the fact that these groups are American draws a crowd," Fr. Dan told me, "and some of the techniques they are using to get converts are absolutely atrocious." Some American missionaries were using what could be called "lollipop evangelism." They would buy off the Romanian kids by offering them candy, gum, and crayons. Some missionary groups even were raising money in America for Romanian relief and then using it to say to people, "If you join us, we'll give you a monthly stipend to help you out economically."

Fr. John Reeves of the Orthodox Church in America was also at the conference, and he volunteered to go. Father Dan asked if I'd be willing to go along. "With the blessing of our Metropolitan, and if we can work out the schedule," I told him, "count me in."

Laying the Plans

Soon after the conference ended, Fr. Dan got the blessing of the Patriarch of Romania and Bishop Nathaniel, the Romanian bishop in America. Father John received approval from Metropolitan Theodosius, I received the go-ahead from Metropolitan Philip, and the wheels began to turn.

Two or three months before the actual trip, Fr. Dan called me to say they were beginning to feel the need to form two teams instead of just one, and they were looking for names. Father Gregory Rogers from Gary, Indiana, came immediately to mind. He had been over to India the previous Christmas and preached to crowds of up to twenty thousand people. So I threw his name into the hat, as well as that of Fr. David Ogan, a former Assembly of God pastor, now a priest in California.

In the end there were two teams. One team was Fr. David and myself with Fr. Dan Suciu acting as our interpreter. (I discovered something very important about interpreters. When you're preaching the Gospel, they can't just interpret words; they've got to preach what you say with the power of the Holy Spirit or it doesn't work. Thanks be to God, both of our interpreters were highly gifted preachers.)

The other team was composed of Fr. Gregory Rogers and Fr. John Reeves. Their interpreter was Archimandrite Roman Braga, one of the most saintly men I've ever met. In the 1950s Fr. Roman had been arrested and held in a communist prison in Romania for eleven years for teaching the Bible to children. He hadn't been back to his homeland since he being exiled twenty-six years before. The emotion Fr. Roman felt at being able to go back home—not just to visit, but to preach the Gospel to his people—was unbelievable.

To jump ahead of my story, on our last day in Romania we were on national television—which is especially significant because there was only one channel in Romania—and Fr. Roman gave an impassioned talk. Of course it was all in Romanian, but Fr. Dan later told us that what he said was essentially, "I went into a communist prison camp knowing Orthodoxy out of the books. I walked out having it in my heart." He fervently urged the people to go all out in their Orthodox Christianity. This man was an apostle of Christ and proved to be a wonderful addition to the team.

With what seemed to be an absolute minimum of hassles or headaches, I found myself seated aboard a Lufthansa Airlines flight from New York via Frankfurt, preparing to touch down at the Bucharest International Airport for fifteen packed-itinerary days in Romania. What an experience awaited us!

A Preacher's Paradise

The thing that amazed me the most as I traveled across Romania was the tremendous interest in the Orthodox Faith. Wherever we went, we found ourselves preaching to great crowds of attentive listeners. It was a preacher's paradise. No matter how long we talked, they were ready for more.

The first night we spoke in Romania, ten thousand people showed up for an open-air service held at the site of a soon-to-be-built Orthodox church in the city of Satu Mare. (We spoke to thirty-five thousand people at a monastery later that weekend. Father Gregory and Fr. John spoke to a crowd of one hundred thousand at another monastery.) At Satu Mare we had ten percent of the city out to hear us the first night. The mayor, himself an Orthodox Christian, showed up for services along with his family. It was like the Book of Acts. If we had stayed for a week, I have no doubt that half to three-quarters of the town would have turned out for services.

Why? For one thing, you don't go home in Romania and watch *Monday Night Football* or *The Tonight Show* on TV. In the US we have so many cushy amusements that we consider our religious services to be an annoying interruption. But there was more to it than that. To see what it's like when Orthodoxy is the faith of the land, go to Romania, where it is embedded in the culture.

When I originally asked for permission from Metropolitan Philip to go on this trip, he wrote me a letter with a little barb that I really liked. He said, "Of course you have my permission. Then I want you to do in America what you are going to be doing in Romania." That's legitimate. Of course, we can't get crowds of thirty-five thousand or a hundred thousand in North America—yet!

As I looked out on the sea of faces that showed up, I found myself wondering if the way we could impact America with the Gospel would be to send people to Romania to bear witness to Christ. Then they could visit us, sharing the gift of their faith with us in an exchange of Christian love. One thing was sure. In Romania, they were deeply thrilled to hear the Good News.

A Heart to Work

At one point on our journey, an incident took place that for me epitomized the heart of the Romanian Orthodox people. We had finished a series of meetings in the city of Târgu Mureş (highlighted by free television coverage from the local station that gave our preaching stops national TV exposure) and were driving to the monastery of St. John the New at Suceava. Unexpectedly the driver said, "By the way, in this next town there is a unique situation."

It seems the people of this area had only a pitiful little church building in town that looked something like a rusted-out World War II gas can with a steeple on top. (The driver was right—when I saw it I thought it might be the ugliest church I'd ever seen in my life!) The people had begged their priest for a new church, but he was old and didn't want the responsibility of a building project on his hands, so he kept refusing. The people told him: "We'll take full responsibility. We'll do the work. Just let us take care of everything." Still, the old priest simply wouldn't budge.

Finally the parishioners came up with a plan. They gave the priest some money for a three-week vacation—an offer he gladly accepted. What they didn't tell him was that by the time he got back, the foundation of a new church building would already be in place, with some of the supports erected. Eventually the priest retired, and the people built an incredibly gorgeous church to replace the gasoline can.

When we drove through this town, we asked the driver to stop so we could look for ourselves and meet the people he had been telling us about. We went into the church and found some people up on the roof putting up plaster and shingles. There was also a man and woman running a cement machine down below. It reminded me of the Book of Nehemiah, where the Scriptures say the people had a mind to work. These people were not rebellious. They were not disobedient. They simply wanted a decent church.

A man and wife were in charge of this project—a modern-day Aquila and Priscilla—and they were working along with everybody else. They had taken time off their jobs, and they were helping to support the work financially. I'd never seen anything like it in my life. The man insisted we come over to his house. Of course, we were already a little behind schedule, so we said we would, but only briefly. We sat in their house and chatted through the interpreter until we finally had to leave—with hugs and tears. All of us felt we had to do something, so we gave them all the money we could afford.

The people of Romania are gifted with very big hearts. Years of unbelievable privation and suffering under the communist regime failed to stamp out the flame of faith in these people. They waiting expectantly for God to perform miracles and revitalize the nation. It was a life-changing experience for me.

The Good, the Bad, and the Ugly

When we first got to Romania, two Americans asked Fr. Roman Braga for help in getting through customs. He politely asked them, "Oh, what brings you to Romania? Are you coming on vacation? Are you tourists?"

They said, "No, we're here to Christianize Romania. We hear it is a pagan nation." Tragically, as Fr. Dan had warned me at our Department of Missions and Evangelism Conference, this is a typical approach from Western Christians. The Romanian Orthodox believers both there and here in America deeply resent that attitude. Yes, there's a lot of work to be done. However, a high percent of the Romanian people still claim to be Orthodox.

In stark contrast to the dismal picture of paganism and superstition painted by Protestant groups trying to raise funds here in America, we found a country that, despite years of communist oppression and attack, still exhibited an incredibly rich underpinning of Christian spirituality. This foundation was found in the fervor of renewed faith springing up among the Romanian people after the demise of the communist regime. It was also to be found on a deeper level—the ancient Orthodox spirituality that permeated the Church at its very roots.

We visited many wonderful monasteries in Romania, some of which were just being reestablished after years of forced closures by the communists. These monasteries and the Spirit-filled, joyous monks and nuns we encountered within them renewed my vision for the Orthodox Christian faith.

At the ancient monastery of Sihastria, we had an audience with the most revered holy man in Romania, Fr. Elie Cleopa. Father Cleopa was eighty-one years old at the time, yet had the countenance of someone forty years younger. He never looked directly at us as he talked, yet there was an expression of great peace and joy on his face.

Father Cleopa told us of his life as a hermit in the wilderness for nine and one-half years and talked about times when his "good friends"—the deer and the bears—helped to provide him with his daily needs. Like the Russian St. Seraphim of Sarov, he lived in total harmony with the wildlife during this time. During the last four years of his isolation, a kind forest ranger began taking the risk of bringing him a bag of potatoes each month, and he inevitably shared even this meager food with his animal friends.

As we talked with Fr. Cleopa about the story of Americans turning to the Orthodox Faith, I mentioned our own journey as the American Evangelical Orthodox Mission (AEOM). Repeatedly he blessed us saying, "May heaven consume you." There was no doubt in his mind that the message of this return to Orthodoxy would be powerfully used in America and in Romania as well, where so many were harassing the Romanian believers with contradictory and confusing teachings.

What a wonderful visit we had with this man of God. It was indeed a humbling, yet intensely rewarding, experience to meet with him for the short time we had together.

Hitting the Streets

My favorite day on the trip was the day we went to the town of Rădăuți. In contrast to the other stops along the way, almost no advance work had been done on the part of the ecclesiastical leaders to prepare for our coming to this area. In fact, we arrived at the monastery of Putna, where we were to lodge, only to find out the bishop had forgotten even to tell them we were coming.

After sizing up the situation the next morning, we said to each other, "If we're going to have a crowd here tonight, we'll have to go out and find it." Some of the monks got involved and started to put together hand-lettered posters announcing the meeting. We had plenty of literature to distribute. The Romanian episcopate in America had translated and printed in Romanian fifty thousand of each of three Christian booklets by Conciliar Press (predecessor to Ancient Faith Publishing). Armed with signs, booklets, and monks, we set off to shake the bushes in the outlying villages to try to secure a crowd for the night's service.

When we hit the first village, we immediately went out into the streets and started talking to people. As the people noticed a crowd forming, they started coming out of their houses. We preached very briefly through the interpreter, passed out literature, and invited them to services that night.

George the Quick (that's what we nicknamed our speed-prone driver) was a young deacon. Deacon George was absolutely the worst driver I have ever ridden with. He made the blind cartoon character Mr. Magoo look like a limousine chauffeur. In the course of one drive we nearly had two head-on collisions. No matter how loudly the rest of us would protest as he drove from place to place, the correction would last for maybe an hour and then he'd go back to his old ways.

But George the Quick had his good points as well. He loved to get out there and mix it up with people. He was a little reserved at first, but the more we started in on street evangelism, the more he came alive. He began telling everybody to show up at night to hear about the Gospel and the need to follow Christ. He must have passed out thousands of booklets.

We went from village to village and then moved on into town, where we started distributing literature in the marketplace. We kept telling everyone, "Cathedral, six o'clock! Cathedral, six o'clock!" It was like my old days on American campuses working for Campus Crusade for Christ. At one point, a group of guys from Ukraine came up to us, looking like they were part of a motor-cycle gang—leather jackets, shirts with three or four buttons open at the top, hairy chests, the works. Father David immediately went over to talk to them. Of course he invited them all to services that night. I was just hoping he wasn't going to get mugged.

In the end, we had a crowd of about seven hundred people show up for Vespers—including the Ukrainian bikers, who were sitting in the front row of the cathedral. Father David gave his testimony. I was to preach that evening. As I started, curiosity got the better of me, and I asked, "How many of you are here tonight because we talked with you today and gave you the literature?" Probably forty or fifty percent of the people raised their hands. The priest later told me the actual numbers were more like seventy-five per-cent. After the years of political oppression, people were too fear-ful to raise their hands or to single themselves out in a crowd.

Homeward Bound

As we flew out of Bucharest to return home, we talked of planning another trip to Romania. Father John Reeves wanted to go back immediately. I was ready, too, except for one thing: it took me a month to recover from the trip! The schedule was intense. It was hot. We often found ourselves standing in the baking sun, preaching in ninety-degree heat for an hour and a half at a time. There was often no running water, no air conditioning, and certainly no Holiday Inn to pop into to cool off for a couple of hours. By the end of the trip, my energy was completely drained.

Despite that, the Romanian trip was enormously fulfilling. The Christians there asked us to come back and bring others. Campus ministry had great potential. We had only to wear Western clothes and start talking in English and the students would materialize. The doors were wide open.

We found the simpler we made the message, the better. Our message was one of hope: committing ourselves daily to Christ in the life of His Body, the Church. There was more hunger for God in Romania than I had ever seen anywhere in the world, and I left there believing that we who are Orthodox Christians must do everything possible to encourage the spiritual lives of people throughout Eastern Europe and Russia. They are waiting on us to do so.

CHAPTER 18

Cancer

*"God's works are never finished,
And from Him health is
upon the face of the earth."*

One evening, when we lived in our home on Sabado Tarde Road just outside of Santa Barbara, I was watching the evening news on our twelve-inch black-and-white–screen TV that we kept in the kitchen. Part of the newscast was a medical report on the seriousness of melanoma, known better as skin cancer. The presentation included a photo display of how melanoma exhibits itself on the skin. A primary indicator would be a mole about the size of a pencil eraser, outlined with a dark border.

I said to myself, "My goodness, I've got one of those on my shoulder." I remember going into the bathroom, pulling up my shirtsleeve, and checking for it in the mirror. Sure enough, it was a dead ringer for what I'd just seen a moment ago on television. I said to Marilyn, "I think I need to have this thing checked."

I made an appointment the next day with our family physician, Dr. Ballard, and asked him to take a look at it. Immediately, in his office, he excised the mole and sent it off for evaluation to the cancer lab in town. A few weeks passed, and then we were relieved to be told that it had come back benign and was not cancerous.

The following Christmas, we had our Santa Barbara family over for dinner, and by now our son-in-law had completed medical school and residency and was an emergency room doctor at the county hospital in Ventura. I said, "Scott, I want you to take a look at my armpit. It's all swollen."

And he said, "Fr. Peter, you need to make an appointment tomorrow to have that thing examined." I told him of the growth I'd had removed about a year earlier and how it had come back benign, and he said, "You know, I don't care. There's something wrong. You need to see the doctor."

So I made an appointment with an oncologist at the Sansum Clinic in Santa Barbara, and she said, "Let us reexamine that growth." Not a week later, she called back and said, "They missed the diagnosis, and you've got stage-three melanoma," which means that it had gone into my lymph nodes and metastasized and could by now have spread throughout my body. Stage-four melanoma is slam-dunk fatal; in stage three, they give you a fifty-fifty chance of surviving. Not since I'd had nephritis as a teenager had I been faced in such stark terms with my own mortality.

Fortunately, my surgeon, Dr. Dunn, was a committed Roman Catholic Christian and an exceptionally good surgeon. The oncologist made an appointment with him for me, and I went into his office and explained what had transpired thus far. He said, "I'm going to do what's called a needle biopsy on you, which will mean I deaden the area of your left armpit and stick in a needle and test several of the lymph nodes there." As one who does not like to be worked on by a doctor, I hoped the local anesthetic would take, and thank God, it did. I knew what was going on but could not bear to watch.

When he finished, he said, "This biopsy has detected absolutely no cancer, but I'm not buying it. Melanoma's one of the most aggressive cancers known to man, and the only way we fight it is aggressively. I'm going to remove several of your lymph nodes while the anesthetic is still in effect, right here on the spot, and send them to the lab."

He did so, and upon receiving the results, immediately called me back into his office. He said, "Two of them were cancerous, and I have no choice but to remove all of the twenty or twenty-one lymph nodes under your left arm."

So I went in for surgery, and they removed all the lymph nodes under my left arm and left shoulder. It turned out that three of the twenty-two were cancerous. Now the question was: had that cancer spread to other lymph nodes in my other armpit or in my groin? These often are the next nodes that are infected by cancer as it metastasizes throughout your body. Only a thorough examination and possibly more surgery would give the answer to that question.

Of course, as Christians we face these things by simply relying on God and not trying to figure everything out. At this point, three things happened that I believe were orchestrated by God. First, He brought to my mind that verse in Philippians where St. Paul says, "Let your requests be made known to God" (Phil. 4:6). It's a passage that doesn't promise a specific answer, but it promises peace.

I asked myself, "What is it that I really want?" My thoughts went back to my grandparents, living in that old Victorian house on Chicago Avenue in Minneapolis, holding hands on their front porch swing at age seventy-two, whom Marilyn and I came upon as new Christians and college kids. I thought, "I really do want to grow old with my wife." Additionally, my heart's desire was to continue to establish more Orthodox churches around the country.

I prayed to the Lord, "Lord, Your will be done, but if You want to know what I want: I want to live long enough to grow old with Marilyn, and I want to live long enough to start many more Orthodox parishes." At that time, I was somewhere north of fifty.

The second thing that happened after my cancer diagnosis was that people sent me icons of St. Nektarios, the beloved Greek saint who reposed in 1920 and established a famous monastery. In his lifetime, he bore the brunt of incredible and unfair criticism from his fellow Orthodox monks, priests, and even bishops. Saint Nektarios is known throughout the Church as a healer, especially of cancer patients. We received two icons of him in the mail and also a vial of holy water from a fountain near his grave.

Thirdly, I began to rely more heavily on the prayers of other saints, both on earth and in heaven, rather than simply trying to navigate through the health crisis by my own prayers and those of my family. Of course I invoked the prayers of St. Nektarios, asking that he intercede with Christ on my behalf as one facing the possibility of death from cancer. Yet I also invited others within the earthly and heavenly body of Christ to intercede on my behalf.

I began to understand that I did not have to go through this challenge alone, because I was part of the body of Christ. In truth, I prayed very little for myself after my diagnosis, relying instead on the prayers of others to see me through. I realized that if I had taken the burden on myself in private prayer, as I probably would have done twenty years earlier, it would have been very easy for me to focus my attention on my own dilemma rather than on the greater reality of Christ, His Church, and His Kingdom. If one turns inward during times of need, rather than inviting the prayers of others on earth and in heaven, an illness can easily degenerate into a pity party. Instead, we are called to cast all our care upon Him because He cares for us (1 Pet. 5:7).

One of the early responses of friends and even family was, "Why don't you sue the doctor who misdiagnosed your growth?" In my years at Thomas Nelson, I had once been named as a defendant in a lawsuit; the plaintiffs were members of a cult whom we had exposed in one of our books. As the lawsuit unfolded, I soon realized the only people who were going to benefit were the attorneys! Since I had been through that year of very heated depositions, there was no way I wanted to go through that again.

As Christians, we are called to forgive others just as the heavenly Father has forgiven us. If in any way I thought this misdiagnosis was intentional or deliberate, I certainly would have seriously considered a lawsuit. But win, lose, or draw, I knew I would put a doctor through hell on earth and probably ruin his career if I sued him. I'd also put myself through hell on earth if I threw my energy into a court battle. It would almost be as if I were confessing that my hope was in the US civil courts rather than in the King of kings and Lord of lords. I decided there was no way I wanted any mistakes that had been made in my case to be subject to the legal system of America rather than to the mercy and grace of our one true God.

Eventually, after thorough examinations by both my derma-tologist and my oncologist (better known as "the cancer doctor"), it became apparent that they had removed everything and that it was now my job to watch out for "pop-ups," or places on my skin indicating new melanoma growths. Thankfully, as far as my doc-tors could tell, cancer hadn't invaded my internal lymph system, and therefore I had emerged successfully from stage three.

On two occasions after this, a growth appeared on my back that was determined to be a new melanoma; both growths were removed without any cancerous spread. Then in 2010 I noticed a new growth on my lower leg. On an area of my calf that I couldn't see without help from a mirror or from other people, it came into existence quickly and seemed to be something new. Again, through the care of a seasoned dermatologist, that growth was removed, and it was diagnosed as melanoma. This time, the wound was large and unfortunately developed a life-threatening infection. But after six months of treatment and the expertise of many physicians, I was finally declared free of melanoma, at least for the time being.

In working on *The Orthodox Study Bible,* I was taken with a book that wasn't familiar to me in my Protestant days. The Wis-dom of Sirach doesn't appear in modern Protestant Bibles but nonetheless has always been part of the Septuagint text that was used by Christ Himself, as well as by the apostles. When St. Paul declared, "All Scripture *is* given by inspiration of God, and *is* prof-itable for doctrine, for reproof, for correction, for instruction in righteousness" (2 Tim. 3:16), the Scripture to which he referred was the Septuagint, which of course includes the Wisdom of Sirach.

In Chapter 38 of that precious book, which is very similar

in tone to Proverbs, there is a section that the Study Bible titles "Honoring the Physician."

> Honor the physician with the honor due him,
> And also according to your need of him,
> For the Lord created him.
> Healing comes from the Most High,
> And he will receive a gift from the king.
> The physician's skill will lift up his head,
> And he shall be admired in the presence of the great.
> The Lord created medicines from the earth,
> And a sensible man will not loathe them.
> Is not water made sweet by wood
> That its strength might be known?
> And He gave skill to men
> That He might be glorified in His wonders.
> By them He heals and takes away pain,
> A druggist making a compound of them.
> God's works are never finished,
> And from Him health is upon the face of the earth.
>
> My son, do not be negligent when you are sick,
> But pray to the Lord and He will heal you.
> Depart from transgression and direct your hands aright,
> And cleanse your heart from every sin.
> Offer a sweet-smelling sacrifice
> And a memorial of the finest wheat flour;
> And pour oil on your offering, as if you are soon to die.
> And keep in touch with your physician,
> For the Lord created him;
> And do not let him leave you,
> For you need him.
> There is a time when success is also in their hands,

For they will pray to the Lord
To give them success in bringing relief and healing,
For the sake of preserving your life.
He who sins before the One who made him,
May he fall into the hands of a physician.
(Wisdom of Sirach 38:1–15)

Through cancer, I was powerfully reminded that healing is both a sovereign act of God and a human process made possible by skilled medical personnel. Fortunately, as Christians we do not have to choose between the two. Saint Luke, that great writer of the Gospel of Luke and the Acts of the Apostles, was himself a physician. Thus, from that and from the passage in Sirach, God makes it clear that He indeed has raised up physicians just as He does civil servants (Rom. 13) and so many other vocations mentioned throughout the Scriptures.

In Orthodox Christianity, we call this phenomenon *synergism*, which literally means "cooperating with God." God is the Lord and has revealed Himself to us, and certainly it is He who discloses to us His will and accomplishes His miracles. Sometimes He does it supernaturally, but sometimes He does it through the skills of those in the medical profession. Perhaps more often than we realize, it's a combination of both. As one who survived a very lethal form of cancer, I give glory to Him for answering the desire of my heart and the prayers of His saints in seeing me through to what has now become a ripe old age.

CHAPTER 19

A Christian Ending

"They spoke of the glories of the eternal kingdom."

There is a curious difference between modern and ancient views of the Christian life. Today we emphasize the new birth, but the ancients emphasized being faithful to the end. We moderns talk of wholeness and purposeful living, while they spoke of the glories of the eternal Kingdom.

This is not to say the early saints ignored initial conversion, nor does it mean that we today have forgotten about the eternal Kingdom, but there's a sense in which our attention has shifted from the completing of the Christian life to the beginning of it.

The heroes in modern Evangelicalism are contemporary Christians: the famous pastors, authors, evangelists, Bible teachers, or born-again athletes and politicians who are in the limelight with stirring testimonies of dramatic conversions. In days gone by, however, it was those who had finished the course, those who—living still, to be sure—had gone on to glory, who were counted as heroes of the faith.

The classic biblical passage describing how the early Church viewed its heroes is Hebrews 12:1–2. Note the sense of the presence of both these mortals and their immortal Savior:

> *Therefore we also, since we are surrounded by so great a cloud of witnesses, let us lay aside every weight, and the sin which so easily ensnares us, and let us run with endurance the race that is set before us, looking unto Jesus, the author and finisher of our faith, who for the joy that was set before Him endured the cross, despising the shame, and has sat down at the right hand of the throne of God.*

Also, recall that in Hebrews 11, no contemporary believers were singled out for accolades. Everyone in that august assembly had completed the earthly pilgrimage in faithful holiness and had been enrolled in heaven. In the ancient Church, living persons were not sainted. This is not to say that living Christians are not saints—the Scriptures call them such—but the early Christians only designated their godly heroes from the ranks of those who had finished the journey successfully. Simply starting well with the Lord was not enough.

Do we not begin to get a message here? Remaining faithful to Christ over a lifetime is essential and of eternal importance in God's sight. A spectacular conversion or a glowing story of deliverance isn't enough. God calls us to be on our feet and in the fight at the final bell.

Epilogue

by Marilyn Gillquist

During Holy Week of 2008, Fr. Peter and I were driving home from Bridegroom Matins at St. Athanasius Orthodox Church in Santa Barbara. He was in a thoughtful mood and told me he felt the Lord had spoken to him during the service. Then, out of the blue, he asked me what I would think of moving to Bloomington, Indiana! Our youngest son, Fr. Peter Jon, his wife Kristina, and their three children had moved to Indiana after graduating from St. Vladimir's Seminary in New York in 2006. They were serving at All Saints Orthodox Church in Bloomington.

Later, in an interview with John Maddex, the CEO of Ancient Faith Radio, Fr. Peter described that moment this way: "On the way home (from the Holy Week service), I said to Marilyn, 'Fasten your seatbelt!' She's always been incredibly willing. In fact, she made the mistake of putting that verse from the Book of Ruth in my wedding ring: '[Whither] thou goest, I will go; [where] thou lodgest, I will lodge. Thy people will be my people, and thy God my God' (Ruth 1:16). She's been tested on that a number of times in our fifty-one years of marriage."

Father Peter was right; I did fasten my seatbelt at first when

I heard his suggestion. Though we both knew Fr. Peter would be retiring soon, the thought of moving to Indiana had never occurred to us. Yet, after many years of knowing my husband, I could tell he was serious.

Fr. Peter had been the Director of Missions and Evangelism for the Antiochian Archdiocese of North America since his ordination and our chrismation into the Orthodox Church in 1987. By the time of this unexpected Holy Week conversation, Fr. Peter was working with two other priests on both the East and West Coasts to establish mission parishes. He believed it would be good to have a mission priest working in the Midwest as well, and he had come to believe that *he* might be that man.

So in 2008, Fr. Peter approached His Eminence Metropolitan Philip and received his blessing for our move to Bloomington, Indiana. We began to prepare for our departure from Santa Barbara, California, our home of thirty years. After living for so long in that beautiful city, leaving our family and our loving church community was not easy. We shed tears, but we believed that this was God's will, and so we felt great peace.

In June of 2009, we moved to Indiana and became "Hoosiers." We lived in a home near our son Fr. Peter Jon and his family. We attended his parish, All Saints Orthodox Church, and enjoyed our new life in the Midwest, coming full circle back to the region where our lives began.

Sometime during the Indiana years, Fr. Peter began to think more seriously about writing another book. As he told John Maddex, "And then, just in the last year or so, [I had] the idea of writing, probably, a last book, and I'd like to call it *The Memories of His Mercy.* . . . I'd start from my youngest memories about how the Lord has been merciful to me and now to us, through those years of searching for the Church, through those years of learning how to be Orthodox and doing the missions and evangelism work, and now through the years of retirement. We continue experiencing His mercy and [we want] to share with other people the faithfulness of God in a way that I hope will motivate them to trust in Him more than they do now."

In May 2012, Fr. Peter and his dear friend Fr. Jon Braun were invited to Jackson, Mississippi, for the celebration of the twenty-fifth anniversary of St. Peter Antiochian Orthodox Church's entrance into the Orthodox faith. This was a precious community of people we had known for over forty years, and we looked forward to seeing them. Though he had been free of cancer for years, my husband had recently been experiencing considerable hip pain, so when we took off for Jackson, the two-day car trip was difficult for him. Nevertheless, he was glad that we went to the celebration; spending the weekend with Bishop Antoun, of the Diocese of Miami, and the clergy and congregation of St. Peter's was memorable for all of us.

After we returned from Mississippi, Fr. Peter kept a routine appointment with his oncologist in Bloomington. The doctor expressed concern, saying it was apparent to her that there were significant changes in the test results since Fr. Peter's last CAT scan. She scheduled additional biopsies, and when the results arrived, they revealed that Fr. Peter had stage-four metastatic cancer.

We contacted all our family with the news. Quickly, it became apparent that Fr. Peter was very ill. June 10, 2012, was his last Sunday liturgy at All Saints. Father Peter announced to the congregation that the cancer had returned and that it was terminal. In the next few days our loving church community offered up prayers, calls, cards, and food. My husband's condition grew worse, and Fr. Peter Jon called his five siblings to tell them to come soon, as their dad's condition was deteriorating rapidly.

Greg and Jennifer and their five children were the first to arrive, all the way from Alaska. The four sisters—Wendy, Ginger, Terri, and Heidi—flew in from California. Brothers Greg and Fr. Peter Jon greeted their sisters at the airport, and the six adult siblings embraced one another in an unforgettable group hug.

On Wednesday, June 20, Fr. Peter was admitted to the hospital, and our children took turns spending the night with him. The following Sunday afternoon he was tired and in pain. Our four daughters sat quietly with him so he could sleep. Suddenly he opened one eye and asked, "What are you—a bunch of Quakers?" They all laughed, thankful their dad still had his sense of humor.

The next day, Fr. Peter's doctors discovered he had blood clots in his left leg, so they scheduled surgery to insert a filter to keep the clots from going to his lungs. As he was about to be wheeled into the operating room, his surgeon and the family gathered around his gurney, and Fr. Peter prayed for the Lord's mercy on his surgery. Thankfully, it was successful.

The next day Dr. John Collis, our dear friend who had performed Fr. Peter's back surgery years earlier, drove in from Ohio for a final visit. The two friends reminisced and talked about the *Orthodox Study Bible* project, which Dr. Collis and his wife Helen had supported.

On Wednesday, June 27, the family met with Dr. Joyce, the oncologist. She talked about the options for Fr. Peter, including

Hospice House, and we made the decision to transfer my husband there by ambulance. We found it to be a gift from God, as it was a beautiful facility and better than anything we could have imagined.

Back before Fr. Peter's final diagnosis, we had planned to host dear friends Rich and Ursula Wagner; Rich was the best man at our wedding, and we'd been looking forward to our reunion, never expecting it would be our last as a foursome and held at the Hospice House. Rich and Ursula's presence brought us great comfort and encouragement.

During Fr. Peter's last week, our daughters bought their dad a Reuben sandwich from a local restaurant, paired with a root beer float—his favorite treat. Obviously pleased, Fr. Peter announced to the family, "You treat me so well. I should be at death's doorstep more often!" Fr. Peter's humor and courage reminded us of his father, Parker, who could always make us smile.

On Thursday, June 28, after a Vesperal Liturgy for Ss. Peter and Paul, Fr. Peter Jon brought his dad Holy Communion. Our daughter Terri and her husband, Dr. Scott Speier, were with him. As Fr. Peter was about to receive communion, he stopped Fr. Peter Jon and said, "Wait!" Father Peter Jon stepped back. His dad said, "I have a question for my doctor." His son-in-law Scott stepped over. Father Peter said his leg was numb "because I have a tumor," and Dr. Speier said, "Yes."

Fr. Peter said, "Okay, I'm ready now."

That Holy Communion was to be Fr. Peter's last food.

The next day was June 29, Fr. Peter's feast day, the Feast of Ss. Peter and Paul. Fr. Peter suffered and was in pain on this day. We were reminded of the kontakion for the feast:

You have taken to Yourself, O Lord, the firm and God-
proclaiming heralds, the Chief Apostles,
for the enjoyment of Your blessings and for repose;
for You have accepted their labors and death as above
all sacrifice, O You Who alone know the secrets of our
hearts.

We tried to pray and comfort him, but it was a difficult time. That evening Fr. Peter suddenly opened his eyes; about a minute later the door to his room opened, and Fr. Gordon Walker appeared. Fr. Gordon and Fr. Peter warmly greeted one another. Through our tears we embraced Fr. Gordon, clinging to him as one of Fr. Peter's dearest friends and one of the original men in the group who had left Campus Crusade in search of the historical Church. Fr. Gordon opened his Bible and wept as he read Romans 8 to us:

For I am persuaded that neither death nor life, nor
angels nor principalities nor powers, nor things present
nor things to come, nor height nor depth, nor any other
created thing, shall be able to separate us from the love of
God which is in Christ Jesus our Lord. (Rom. 8:38–39)

We needed him and were grateful for his presence, along with that of Elijah Reynolds, the grandson-in-law who had driven him all the way from his parish in Franklin, Tennessee.

On Saturday, June 30, more visitors came. Fr. Gordon continued to spend time at Fr. Peter's bedside. Ann Thomas, our dear friend from Ohio, traveled to see my husband one last time. There were phone calls with Fr. Jon and Mary Ellen Braun, longtime friends who were also part of our original Campus Crusade group. Later, Fr. Jon, Fr. Gordon, and Fr. Peter had a three-way conversation via speakerphone; the three lifetime friends reminisced and gave thanks to God. We were also grateful for the presence of Fr. Nabil Hanna, who drove from Indianapolis to help, encourage, and give wise advice as the end came near.

Finally, Fr. Gordon heard Fr. Peter's last confession.

On Sunday, July 1, 2012, the Feast of Ss. Cosmos and Damian, Fr. Peter's cough turned to a rattle after a restless night. Lloyd and Barbara George, Fr. Peter Jon's in-laws, said Matins prayers with us; hearing Lloyd chant the prayers was a great comfort to Fr. Peter. Fr. Gordon came to say good-bye and pray with us. More family arrived after the Divine Liturgy at church, and we spent the afternoon singing to Fr. Peter, glad to drown out the rattle in his breathing with our music.

Several grandchildren called to say their goodbyes to their "Gee Gee." When the phone was put to his ear, the rattling stopped and was replaced with quiet sighs as he listened to their voices. Late in the afternoon, daughter-in-law Kristina came to tell us that Fr. James Ellison, one of Fr. Peter's close friends, was on his way from Illinois. According to his GPS, he would arrive a little before nine-thirty p.m.

When the nurse checked on Fr. Peter, his breathing had become labored. She suctioned his throat and noted that his oxygen level was at sixty percent. His hands were beginning to turn blue. Wendy was alone with her dad and was singing to him. The rattling grew very loud, and it seemed he was struggling to breathe. Wendy prayed fervently, blessing his throat, neck, and forehead with an oil-drenched cotton swab from a myrrh-streaming icon she carried in her reliquary cross necklace. She placed her cross and Virgin Mary pendant on his inner arm where it lay outstretched on the bed. At around nine p.m., my husband's hands were pink again and warm. The nurse checked his oxygen level. It was ninety percent.

At nine-twenty p.m. Wendy was standing at the door of the room saying goodbye to Kristina, who was leaving. I was sitting on the couch at the foot of the bed with Terri. Fr. Peter suddenly drew in his breath forcefully and exhaled for the last time. All at once, there was a peaceful quiet in the room—and no more rattle.

Wendy stepped out into the hallway and motioned to Fr. Peter Jon and Dr. Scott Speier to come. As they entered the room, my husband exhaled two times, his last earthly breaths. Scott checked my husband's pulse, and Fr. Peter Jon simultaneously picked up his service book to begin reading the prayers for the departing of the soul.

We gathered around the bedside, Wendy and Terri on each side of me with their arms around me. My faithful dog Oggie walked over to the bed, licked Fr. Peter's hand, and then lay down on the floor beside him. At the foot of the bed, Fr. Peter Jon and Lloyd George were praying, and Fr. James Ellison—who had pulled into the parking lot at nine-twenty p.m.—joined them.

Across the room was a shelf holding votive candles in front of seven icons that Fr. Peter Jon had brought to Hospice House: Christ; the Holy Theotokos; St. Peter, holding the keys to the Kingdom; Ss. Peter and Paul, embracing; St. Nectarios; St. Panteleimon; and the Holy Unmercenaries Cosmos and Damien. When Fr. Peter drew his last breath, all the candles went out, except the two in front of the icons of St. Peter and of Ss. Peter and Paul. By the time we finished the prayers and songs, the remaining two candles had flickered and then gone dark.

Wendy and Terri called family members to tell them of Fr. Peter's passing. When the funeral home removed his body, the priests and family followed, singing the Trisagion Hymn as Fr. Peter was transferred to a waiting vehicle. Heidi, who had returned to California due to work responsibilities, joined in via Terri's mobile phone as the family sang. The acoustics in the hallway amplified the voices, and Heidi asked if there was a choir there. Terri replied, "No, just the family." Later I thought, perhaps there *was* a choir, an angelic choir, joining us! All things are possible.

Then it was time to attend to all the final details and say our earthly farewells to our beloved husband, father, grandfather, and friend. When it became apparent that his end was near, Fr. Peter had said to his son Fr. Peter Jon, "We need to talk." There were some priestly things Fr. Peter wanted him to take care of, and the number one item was his vestments.

Fr. Peter Jon said, "Yes, dad, you want to be buried in your blue vestments." Fr. Peter, senior, answered, "No, I want you to have them." These blue vestments were especially precious because the beautiful fabric had come from Syria and they were a gift from Metropolitan Philip.

Fr. Peter repeated to his son, "I want you to have them."

"Are you sure?" Fr. Peter Jon asked.

"Absolutely," his dad replied.

"Then what are you going to be buried in?"

His dad answered, "What do you think, Father?"

Fr. Peter Jon said, "I want you to be buried in my Paschal white vestments." And that is what happened.

Upon the arrival at Holy Trinity Greek Orthodox Cathedral

for the funeral, Bishop Anthony told the priests to wear their green vestments because it was the season of Pentecost. Father Peter Jon said, "Your Grace, if I may, my father is vested in white."

Bishop Anthony said, "Well then, we will dress to match—in white."

Bishop Anthony and clergy at Fr. Peter's funeral, July 6, 2012, Holy Trinity Greek Orthodox Cathedral, Carmel, IN

Father Peter loved his country, and it seemed appropriate that he was laid to rest during the Fourth of July week. His first services were at our son's parish in Bloomington, Indiana, on July 4 and 5, and then his body was transferred to Indianapolis for a Trisagion Service and Divine Liturgy, with His Grace Bishop Anthony of the Diocese of Toledo and the Midwest presiding. On Friday, July 6, 2012, over thirty priests concelebrated with the bishop at Holy Trinity Greek Orthodox Church in Indianapolis. Tributes poured in from around the world, and hundreds of people posted memories and condolences on the All Saints Bloomington website. We rejoiced and we wept as we read of how Father's life and words had touched and encouraged so many.

One particular tribute to Fr. Peter stands out to me. The Very Rev. Joseph Copeland of Holy Cross Orthodox Church in Yakima, Washington, said, "I am always thankful to God for Fr. Peter's vision and enduring love. In large part we are where we now are, in Christ's Holy Church, because of Fr. Peter. We are so blessed because of his zeal for the True Faith and that of the men with him who charted such a bold course.

"The day that Fr. Peter reposed," he added, "our iconographer from Serbia was working on the 'Heavenly Liturgy' in our parish dome. He heard of Father's death and spontaneously wrote on the cloth being carried by one of the angels, 'O Lord, remember Thy servant the priest Peter,' in Church Slavonic.

"God willing," concluded Fr. Joseph, "our walls will echo that petition until the Lord returns."

Father Peter's dear friend Fr. Bill Olnhausen, retired priest from St. Nicholas Orthodox Church in Cedarburg, Wisconsin, said in his homily on July 8, after Fr. Peter had been laid to rest:

As for Fr. Peter, thank God for him and all he did for us. He was a great friend to us. He still is. We now have a powerful intercessor in heaven. I have found myself already saying, 'Fr. Peter, pray for us.' Over his body Friday morning at the funeral I heard a priest friend whisper, 'Fr. Peter, pray for us.' That's how it starts. It could be that Fr. Peter's greatest work is just beginning. We will never forget you, Fr. Peter Gillquist. 'Memory eternal' indeed!

Tributes

Father Gordon Walker was one of the original Campus Crusade men who eventually formed the Evangelical Orthodox Church. He was ordained to the holy priesthood and assigned to lead St. Ignatius Orthodox Church in Franklin, Tennessee, where he ministered until his repose on July 23, 2015. One of Fr. Peter's closest friends, Fr. Gordon offered this reflection at Fr. Peter's memorial service.

I count it such a privilege, and yet a sad privilege, that His Grace Bishop Anthony would have asked me to bring this homily today. Fr. Peter and I have known each other and labored together to serve the Lord for over fifty years now, and that's a long time. You get to know one another pretty well. You sleep in the same bed on some of the trips we went, you travel in close quarters, you see the heart of a person. I felt I got to see inside the heart of Peter Gillquist, truly a man who loved God, who loved his family, who loved those that he served and that served with him. So it's not been easy. I'm older than he, so, Father, you jumped the gun, went ahead of me here. By nature, he should be preaching at my funeral.

But we are so thankful for this man of God, because his influence and the power of his life will continue to go like ripples in a pond or in a lake, all out into the heavenly Kingdom here on earth. I can't speak for the Kingdom in heaven. I'm looking forward to investigating that someday.

As I was trying to think what can I say, what kind of passage can I preach from that would in a sense honor this man and his life, and the only thing I could come up with was what we call the Great Commission, and I'd like to read these words to you, from Matthew 28:16–20.

> *Then the eleven disciples went away into Galilee, to the*
> *mountain which Jesus had appointed for them. When*
> *they saw Him, they worshiped Him.*

This is after the Resurrection, and they really do understand who He is at this point. It says:

> *They worshiped Him; but some doubted.*

Uh-oh. Thomas is still in the group. And by the way, the only saint's name I have is Thomas. My middle name is Thomas.

> *And Jesus came and spoke to them, saying, "All*
> *authority has been given to me in heaven and on earth.*
> *Go therefore and make disciples of all the nations,*
> *baptizing them in the name of the Father and of the*
> *Son and of the Holy Spirit, teaching them to observe all*
> *things that I have commanded you; and lo, I am with*
> *you always, even to the end of the age." Amen.*

Well, that passage does honor this great man that we're here to honor today, because he loved that passage and he lived that passage. I was sort of amazed that even after he was supposed to have retired, he still was doing all he could, right up to the very last.

Let me say a few words about Thomas, who was in this group. Some of you have heard me talk about Thomas—I don't know a lot about him; I just did a little bit of research on him—but these were some important points about his life, because in saying these things I think you'll see how I am attempting to apply this to Fr. Peter's life.

Thomas was one of the apostles who went outside the Roman Empire to preach. There were only two of them. The other was Andrew. The other ten of the twelve all preached within the boundaries of the Roman Empire. So going outside the boundaries was going out where the heathen were, wild tribes that might turn on you in a moment for reasons you wouldn't even know about, and your life was in constant danger out in the outside world, outside of the Roman world. But St. Andrew and St. Thomas both felt that was their calling, and they spent most of their lives doing this work.

I got some of this information from a Greek layman who has spent many years researching the lives of Thomas and Andrew, and he spoke of the places that Thomas had gone. It appears that Andrew and Thomas went through Russia, or part of Russia, northern Europe, and North Africa. Thomas's life and journeys are recorded in the Syriac document, *The Acts of Thomas*. Thomas traveled a vast area on foot and by ship. It is recorded that he walked across the huge Parthian empire, on foot all the way, and that empire embraced Iraq, Iran, Turkmenistan, Afghanistan, and Pakistan, which borders on India. It appears he may have briefly visited China, but then he went to India, where he had his greatest ministry.

Finally, at the end of his life, Thomas was stoned and stabbed to death by a Brahmin priest on a mountain outside of Mylapore, India, on December 21, AD 72. It is reported that Thomas had over one thousand converts from all four castes in India. That was almost unbelievable and unheard of. You could reach the poor castes, but you couldn't reach the wealthy and the powerful. He reached into all aspects of the life of India, and the Church in India had a great early history. It's still there. We need to pray that these places where the apostles first traveled will all be reignited with the power of the Holy Spirit and with the true Church, through the instrumentality of the true Church.

I believe that this is so much of what Fr. Peter felt. When we started out, there were seven of us that were meeting together four times a year. That started in 1972. In 1979, one of the men left us—and that was a heartbreaking experience for me. Then we went on with the remaining six to continue to have meetings four times a year for six days at a time, wherever we could get a place to meet. We had some amazing experiences and went to some amazing places in those meetings. At some point, and I don't remember the precise date, after we had chosen the name, the Evangelical Orthodox Church—and I think this was in the year '79, when we met at Boulder Creek, Colorado—and we decided that Fr. Peter would be our presiding bishop, and that was a very wise choice. It was the choice of the Holy Spirit.

He was the youngest among us. That was the natural thing to do. There's a scripture that says that the young will lead the elders. And so we felt that this was a good thing, to choose him, and a unanimous decision among all the other five, other than himself. He led us well. He was a good organizer.

We had started the meeting with some tension, and I told my wife Mary Sue, "I'm not sure but what this will be my last meeting with these men." This California crowd was scaring me with their talks about *authority in the Church* and things like that, and I was the anti-authority guy.

When we got there, Fr. Richard and I got into a bit of a tiff at the very beginning of the meeting. After about five minutes of this—and it was intense—the thought occurred: "You can go down to the bunkhouse"—we were on this sort of a camp area up there, a Christian camp area—I said, "I can go down to the bunkhouse, throw my things back in the suitcase, and I can hitchhike back to Denver, and I've got a ticket: I know I could transfer and fly home. I don't have to be here."

And when I stood up to do that, a voice said, "*Sit down!*" Now, my father spoke like that. He didn't use many words when he wanted me to do what I knew I needed to do. So I sat down. Within minutes—I would say no more than five—it was obvious. Here there were six of us only in this meeting, but the Holy Spirit came into the room in some way that I cannot explain, but it was a powerful experience of the presence of the Holy Spirit.

From that meeting on, we never had any more arguments. We had discussions, sometimes even debates, but not arguments—because we were all on the same side, pulling for the same goal, and ultimately we knew the Lord was with us.

There were times when we wondered, "Is this going to survive? Will anything good come out of all of this?" As the years went by, ultimately, we did make contact with Metropolitan Philip after we had made a trip to Istanbul to meet with the Ecumenical Patri-archate, and it was sort of "nice to see you, but there's no oppor-tunity here." That was the sad part about our visit there, but when we came back and continued to pray for God's guidance, through a set of what I know could only be called miraculous events, we were given opportunity to meet with Metropolitan Philip.

Finally—and I'm really abbreviating a lot of things, but finally we came to the point that by this time we had about thirty of us of the younger men who were pastoring, most of them, house-churches—and I'm looking out at the faces of people who were in those house-churches or led those house-churches—and they were scattered about the United States and Canada and Alaska. It was amazing that when we finally met together with the Metro-politan at Englewood, New Jersey, here more than thirty men—I don't remember the exact number, but we were able to plead our case with the Metropolitan.

However, there were forces that didn't think we should come in, because we looked like a bunch of gringos or rebels or some-thing that didn't know what we were about [to] those who just saw the exterior. Metropolitan Philip saw our hearts, and as it appeared that he was going to make the decision to have another meeting, I stood and said, "Your Eminence, if you don't receive us, where will we go? We've been everywhere else. We've sought, we've knocked on all the other doors." There was this long pause, and then he just held out his arms, and he said, "Gentlemen, wel-come home." And that opened the door for us, and I can't tell you what a joy filled our hearts.

Father Peter had many meetings with the Metropolitan. They were very, very close. From that point on, all kinds of things began to happen. I pray to God that, much like the early apostles, there will be many, many doors open. Even after the death of the twelve, there were great numbers who stepped forward to carry the Gospel of Christ. Perhaps now there are just two of us left of that original group, but there are many others that I look at up here among these priests and deacons, and I know there is a great future ahead for our archdiocese and for all of Orthodoxy in North America. I believe that the Orthodox Church in North America can become a tremendous light that will attract those who have soft hearts to the true faith.

So let us not get weary. Let's not lose heart. When someone who was truly a giant among us—Fr. Peter is truly in that category—when they pass on, it seems like it leaves a huge hole in our ranks, but the truth is: Christ is with us. *He* is with us. His prayers are with us, and we *will* be able to continue on with His support and that of many in the heavenly Kingdom who have left our churches already.

We have had many to pass on. Fr. Harold Dunaway was an apostle in Alaska and a powerful instrument for God in establishing that wonderful church there at Eagle River and all the missions that have come out of it. There's virtually not a parish among us that has not started other missions. I think virtually all of them have. Not only we, but many others who were not a part of this EOC crowd, this Evangelical Orthodox Church—you know, the Metropolitan loved that name. And he still, to this day, when he sees any of us, he calls us "the Evangelicals." It's a beautiful name; it's a name we should treasure and hold dear.

God is not through with us yet. He's not through with Fr. Peter yet. He has a lot more that he's going to do here in our nation, and not just in America: in other nations of the world, as this Good News of true, living Orthodoxy spreads—and it will spread. Thank God that we who are in this room today, this beautiful parish that has allowed us to come for this meeting— thank God. We will see things that we didn't dream could happen. I'm so thankful for His Grace Bishop Anthony, and what a joy it is that he has been one of those that God has raised up. We need more bishops like you, Your Grace. Thank you for giving me this privilege. In the name of the Father and the Son and the Holy Spirit. Amen.

Father Dan Suciu, the priest who traveled with Fr. Peter to Romania, wrote this letter to Marilyn after Fr. Peter's repose.

Dear Marilyn,

Thank you for sending us a picture with Fr. Peter's grave. It helped a lot to see his "planting ground"; we go to the graves of our loved ones like farmers who go to the fields to check on the crop. They seed with faith, they care for their fields with faith, they hope and wait faithfully for the crop, knowing that the day will come when they will rejoice at the harvest.

There is a story which I used a lot throughout my ministry and which I call "The potato story." I would like to share it with you.

Back home, during the Communist economy and its deficiency, our parents had to produce additional fruit and vegetables wherever they could to help supplement their income.

Every fall they would harvest a bunch of potatoes, among other things, from our large gardens. In the cold basement intended for this purpose, they would carefully store the potatoes to be consumed by us and the animals on one side and then the seed potatoes on the other.

By late February–March, there were no potatoes left in the bunch we consumed, the potatoes were very expensive in the store, and, as a child at about nine years of age, I used to crave home fries desperately, but, we couldn't afford them.

That year, I began to help more with the outdoor chores and, late March, my mom, my dad, my brother and I were about to get ready to plant the potatoes. They brought out the fairly large size potatoes they had saved for seed, and, we started to cut them in 10–12 pieces each, to be planted into the ground.

I remember protesting and saying: "Why can't we make fries from these nice potatoes and eat them, instead of burying them into the ground?" In my mind, it made no sense to bury something you would like to eat so badly.

I still remember my mom telling me: "Danut, you will see how, during the summer, I will send you out with the hoe to dig a couple of potato hills so we can enjoy them; we part with them now to have more of them and enjoy them later."

Sure enough, later on that year, she did send me out to dig a couple of hills and, I was shocked to see that 1% of a potato grew into 10–12 large potatoes; wow!

Oh, during my thirty years of priesthood, I accompanied so many who were hurting so much, to put their loved ones into the ground; it is so hard to part with the body of someone we will miss so much.

But, the Lord became *the fruit* for us, He was planted like *seed* into the ground, He is *the farmer* who waited for the harvest, and, in Him, we have seen the entire process fulfilled and have been overwhelmed by the joy of the harvest.

Because of Him, and in Him, we look at "the planting ground" of Fr. Peter's grave and, beyond the pain of the separation, we see the Day of the Harvest, the Eighth Day of the resurrection of all and its ineffable joy; thus, "the potato hill" is a reminder not of burial, but, of harvest.

May He bless all of you with continued faith, with the conviction that we "look for the Resurrection of the dead and the life of the age to come!"

In His love,

Fr. Dan Suciu

Father Luke and Presbytera Faith Veronis serve a parish of the Greek Orthodox Archdiocese in Webster, Massachusetts; Fr. Luke was one of the priests who joined Fr. Peter for the mission outreach to Romania. He wrote this letter to Marilyn after Fr. Peter's repose.

Dear Presbytera Marilyn,

A "Good Paradise" to our beloved Fr. Peter. May his soul rest in peace among all the saints, and may he be one of our ceaseless prayer warriors interceding for his beloved family, friends, Church community, and world!

What a special husband you had! I'm sure you have received many phone calls, and notes, extolling Fr. Peter, and telling you what a special man he was, and what a great impact he had on so many people's faith. His booming voice, his charismatic spirit, his imposing presence, his down-to-earth humor, his unceasing zeal and passion to share the Gospel with all people, his kindness and friendliness with all, and the list could go on! He was truly a man with so many gifts and talents, and thank God, he strived to use all his gifts for the glory of God!

As a cradle Orthodox, I thank God for his journey into Orthodoxy, and the impact that he has had on our Church here in America! So many people will tell about how their encounter with Fr. Peter enriched their lives and their faith.

Both Faith and I recall his two visits to Albania and the impact he had on our students and the faithful. Not too many people could come to Albania in a cross-cultural setting, for only a few days, and impact the students like Fr. Peter did! And of course, not only were the Albanians blessed, but our whole missionary community was blessed by his presence.

We express our deepest condolences to you, his beloved wife. When I think of the two of you, I think also of my own parents. I always tell my parents that one of the greatest legacies they left us children was that of a wonderful marriage. I know the same can be said of you and Fr. Peter.

We love you, and thank God for you and your witness, as well as thank God for the incredible legacy that Fr. Peter has left us all!

With much love and respect in our Lord Jesus Christ,

Fr. Luke and Presbytera Faith Veronis

Ss. Constantine & Helen Greek Orthodox Church

AGAIN *Interview*

"From Becoming Orthodox to Being Orthodox: An AGAIN interview with Fr. Peter Gillquist" (AGAIN magazine, Vol. 30, No. 1, pp. 6–10)

AGAIN: Fr. Peter, tell us what things looked like back in 1978. What was going on in terms of the early Evangelical Orthodox Church? Who were the early leaders? Give us a feeling for what life was like back in those exciting days. How much of this was hype and how much was a genuine movement of the Holy Spirit?

FPG: Well, as far as we were concerned the whole thing was all very genuine. After having served together with people like Fr. Richard Ballew, Fr. Jon Braun, Fr. Jack Sparks, and Fr. Gordon Walker in Campus Crusade during the sixties, at the beginning of the seventies we began to try to find what we called the New Testament Church. In other words, knowing that we needed to be church and not just parachurch or independent, we began a study through history to try to find where that New Testament Church went. By '78 we were pretty convinced that that Church was the Holy Orthodox Church—the church Rome had left in the eleventh century. Historically it was very clear to us that the Orthodox Church was that Church we read about in the pages of the New Testament.

By 1978 we had formed an order called the New Covenant Apostolic Order, which was a base of fellowship and a working relationship between those of us who were on this pilgrimage. At first we had tried not to be a denomination because we knew the world didn't need another denomination, so we settled for an order. By '78 a number of other men and women had joined us who did not have our common background in Campus Crusade but had the common yearning to find the New Testament Church.

AGAIN: Do you ever miss those early days, the fervor and excitement?

FPG: You know, I don't. We sure had some great times both in Campus Crusade and in the early days of what became the Evangelical Orthodox Church, but those were also days of frustration. All of us were highly committed to evangelism, and yet in being on the pilgrimage we would change, we would accommodate what we were doing to make sure it was consistent with the historic Church, which meant we were in a fairly regular state of flux. It was almost impossible to invite new people on board with us because all we could guarantee them was that ultimately we would be part of the One Holy Catholic and Apostolic Church. But because of the flux it was very difficult to ask them to make a commitment to go on that journey with us. So the seventies really were a decade where we didn't do a lot of evangelism, but mainly did our study of church history to find the fullness of that New Testament faith.

AGAIN: What was the thought behind *AGAIN* magazine and Conciliar Press some 120 issues ago? Why start another publication? What were the goals?

FPG: That's an easy one to answer. Purely and simply our goal was to have a publishing arm that would help teach our people what we were learning about the ancient Christian faith. The magazine started out as a tabloid-size newspaper—not many pages, maybe 16 or 24—and then later became more of a magazine, and if I remember right, we had two colors, then later four-color print. That was the pure and simple purpose behind the whole thing— to be able to put into print the things we were learning to better instruct our people in the midst of this journey.

AGAIN: Some of the folks who were part of the journey in the early days aren't a part of it now. Others appeared interested for a time, but dropped away. What happened?

FPG: It's a sobering thing. A man who was very close to me personally stayed with us on the journey until we came to the place in our study where we saw that the Church viewed the bread and wine of Communion as the body and blood of Christ in a mystery. He simply could not handle that it was anything more than a symbol. So he took his leave in the late seventies. I remember a short time after that I was reading John 6, which is where Jesus teaches extensively that "unless you eat My flesh and drink My blood you have no life in you." At the end of that chapter it says, "Many of His disciples left Him." They simply couldn't handle that bread and wine could be a mystery of the body and blood of Christ. I think that's likely what was the situation here.

Then others left over fear. Some who left us in the early eighties said, "If we become Orthodox they're going to clip our wings, we can't do Bible study, we can't do evangelism," and nothing could be further from the truth. Fast-forward now 21 years after we've been in the Church: we've brought out the *Orthodox Study Bible* New Testament and now just recently the full Old and New Testaments. We've added over a hundred churches to the Archdiocese since we've come in, and seen probably thousands of people embrace the Orthodox faith. So if anything, rather than the Church clipping our wings, we've been working overtime with the blessing of our metropolitan and our other bishops to get this job done. So we're gratified by all that God has done, and by the same token we're very sorry there were those who left us.

By the way, one other thing that will probably be encouraging to pastors and people. That is, Jesus had people leave Him, notably Judas and others. St. Peter lost Ananias and Sapphira. The last letter St. Paul ever wrote was 2 Timothy, and at the end of that book he says things like, "Demas has left me, having loved this present world," "Alexander the Coppersmith did me much harm," and then that really sad verse, "Only Luke [the apostle Luke] is with me." So as he was under house arrest in Rome, Luke was there and that was about it; and though the vast majority of his disciples continued on faithfully, some had left him. It's never a happy thing, but it's seemingly the way life in the Church is. You win a lot of battles and you lose a few.

AGAIN: If you had a time machine and could go back to 1978, what would you say to this group of two thousand evangelicals who were moving toward Orthodoxy? If you were preaching to them, what encouragement would you offer? What warnings would you give them?

FPG: It's impossible to look ahead, but in 1978, as I say, we were convinced that the Orthodox Church is that Church we read about in the New Testament. We simply encouraged each other to stay the course. There were things we had learned by '78 that were fully Orthodox, and things we hadn't yet learned.

Looking back, I would say the thing we need to stress today with the converts is the need to learn how the Orthodox Church works—the fancy name for that is ecclesiology. As evangelical Protestants, we were so used to doing our own thing, exercising our independence—a favorite slogan was, "Nobody's going to tell me what to do or what to believe." You just can't live that way as an Orthodox Christian. Because number one, we're all under the lordship of Christ, and secondly, within the Church, as scriptures teach, He has established apostles, prophets, evangelists, pastors, and teachers. In other words, there is authority in the Church, and we are under those God has set in oversight over us, namely our bishops. As early as AD 107 St. Ignatius of Antioch warns us, "Don't do anything in the Church apart from the bishop."

I would have to say this is the hardest thing for a modern-day Christian to understand: that the Church is not some kind of twenty-first–century holy democracy, it's a theocracy. Things are to be done as St. Paul exhorted in Corinthians, "decently and in order." We're not a bunch of independent, isolated Lone Ranger

Christians. And again I think that is the single hardest thing for a modern-day Christian to learn.

AGAIN: Let's go in the other direction. If you stepped into that time machine thirty years ago, returned to the present and spent a week worshipping, evangelizing, sharing in community life in the average Orthodox parish of today, what would your thoughts be on the return trip? Is this what you envisioned it would be in 1978?

FPG: Well, of course the answer is yes and no. Yes in the sense that in the Church we found those doctrines, those precious biblical truths we held dear, many of which we knew as Protestants, many of which we had to learn as Orthodox. But we hadn't yet immersed ourselves, and I use this word advisedly, in the culture of the present-day Orthodox Church. It's interesting the word "culture" comes from the Latin word *cult* or *cultus*, which means worship. What shocked us was the way the Orthodox worshipped. Sitting in 1978 looking out, we found the doctrine and the truths that we held dear, but we were blown away by the difference of the worship. Most every Christian views "normal" worship as what he or she is experiencing. Of course what we were experiencing in 1978 was a lot of spontaneity, very little sense of liturgy at that point, so consequently we felt that was normal. Then, when we opened the doors of the modern-day Orthodox Church and walked in, we were amazed at how intricate, how overwhelming the worship seemed to us, how ancient, how otherworldly—and that's a good word, "otherworldly," but that was the big thing we had to learn that we couldn't have anticipated in 1978.

AGAIN: What would you say are the greatest contributions of the EOC to Christianity at large today? To Orthodoxy?

FPG: It's always hard to evaluate yourself, and in fact there are warnings both in the scripture and in secular writings against that. I would have to say the number one contribution that we made to Orthodoxy in particular, and to Christendom in general, would have to be the publication of the *Orthodox Study Bible*. It's the first time ever that there has been an Orthodox English translation in print of the Septuagint version, the Greek version of the Old Testament, which is the version the Orthodox Church has always used and which is favored by some Christians who are not Orthodox. The text itself is a gift. The notes that accompany the text I think are a significant help to both Orthodox and non-Orthodox, and there are quite a number of people who have become Orthodox through reading the *Orthodox Study Bible* [New Testament, published in 1992].

A second thing we've been able to bring to the Orthodox Church is the spirit of evangelism. It's interesting that in each of our Divine Liturgies on Sunday morning we pray for prophets, evangelists, teachers, martyrs, and so on. The gift of evangelism had largely been lost in the twentieth-century Orthodox Church. And now as we're in the twenty-first century, that gift is being rediscovered. I honestly believe the reason it was in large part lost was the incredible persecution the Orthodox Church has been under, especially for the last 400 years or so, much of it by the Muslim Ottoman Turks, and more modernly by the communist regime in Russia, in which conservative estimates tell us probably 40 million Orthodox believers lost their lives. These things do not make a good context for aggressive, godly evangelism. Thus in our early days of being Orthodox, let's say in the late 1980s, people would say, "Evangelism, that's Protestant." You never hear that anymore in the Orthodox Church, so I think the second gift would be the whole area of evangelism.

Thirdly, I would say Bible teaching-oriented sermons. For a number of reasons—a lack of education of the clergy in some of the old countries; the threat of enemies being present in the church; and the whole phenomenon of immigrants trying to communicate effectively in a new world—these factors and probably others have contributed to preaching getting the short end of the stick. I think I see this changing now in the church of the twenty-first century; I think we've rediscovered the gift of preaching. I thank God for that.

AGAIN: What mistakes were made along the way? If you had it all to do over again, what would you do differently?

FPG: I would say we probably were not good at communicating some of the things that we learned about Orthodoxy that were different from what we knew as Protestants. Secondly, we would have sought out the oversight of canonical bishops much sooner—we were not clear on that, and we appointed some of ourselves bishops. Yet I would have to say that had we not taken that move, we probably wouldn't be in the Church today. St. Paul said, "We see through a glass darkly," and if that's true of that enlightened apostle, how much more is it true of a handful of ex-Campus Crusade guys who were trying to find their way to the Orthodox Church? Those would be a couple of areas that I'd say we could have done better, though honestly, we operated on the insight we had, and therefore I don't see how we could have done these things much differently than we did do them.

AGAIN: One more trip in the time machine. Let's say you've traveled to the year 2038. What do you hope to see when you get out? What would be your greatest hope for the Orthodox Church in North America? Be realistic, but dream a little.

FPG: Well, I don't say this to be funny. The greatest dream I could imagine would be to be seated with the saints at the right hand of God, the Lord having come and received us into His Holy Kingdom. I just can't think of anything greater than that.

If the Lord tarries and does not return by 2038, I would first of all love to see the Orthodox Church worshipping in the language of America rather than the language of the mother countries. I fully understand the frustration of immigrants who get here and don't know English. But the lion's share of worship by then really needs to be in English, and not just for the sake of the Americans who aren't Orthodox, but for the sake of the children of the Orthodox people who are clueless when it comes to the language of the mother country. That would be one thing.

Secondly, I remember when we first discovered the Orthodox Church, before we were even in, and all six of my kids were at home, we'd go on family vacations—we'd drive, maybe on a two-lane highway, through several small towns, and then we'd get back on the freeway. We'd pull through a town and my kids would say, "Dad, there's the Catholic church, there's the Lutheran church, there's the Methodist church, the Baptist, where on earth is the

Orthodox church?" And I'd have to say, "Kids, we're just starting out on the job of evangelizing here in America." But you know, thirty years from now, if we could take that same trip, hopefully you wouldn't have to ask that same question. That would be my goal for the year 2038: that not only would we expand in the cities we're already present in, places like Pittsburgh, Philadelphia, Cleveland, and LA, but that we'd be able to have a number, maybe scores of churches in towns that no one's ever heard of. We've done a few of those, and to be honest, they've done well, but we need to get out into the towns of 50,000 to 100,000 people where there's no Orthodox church, and build communities and see them thrive. This would be my other dream for the year 2038.

AGAIN: Years ago you wrote a book called *Why We Haven't Changed the World*. Why didn't the parachurch movement of the late sixties and seventies change the world? You left that movement in order to be a part of the movement to Orthodoxy. Do you think the Evangelical Orthodox movement has changed the world?

FPG: It wouldn't have done anything, I don't believe, had it not been received into the canonical Church. Because you can't exist apart from the Church of Christ and His apostles and expect to thrive. Even then, "all that live godly in Christ will suffer persecution." When I say "thrive," I don't mean a thrill a minute with the devil asleep, but rather that we're out there in the battle, we win more than we lose.

The reason the parachurch movements haven't changed the world is that the gift of evangelism, as with all spiritual gifts, was a gift given to the Church. Any time you take a gift of the Spirit and try to put it to work outside the care and covering of the Church, you run into difficulty. We all remember back to some of the weird stuff that happened in the charismatic movement, some of the excesses, in the seventies and the years that followed. Also in the area of evangelism. In our parachurch days we were as committed to evangelism as any group of men I know. But if you remember back to the seventies, as we and so many others were out there trying to evangelize, the world not only didn't get better, it got worse—it became less Christian. What we were doing was like the guy who runs around town fathering children and just leaving them on people's doorsteps. The norm is for the local parish to engage in evangelism, and then the fruit of that work becomes a part of the parish. In the parachurch scheme of things you don't have that.

I would say again, 21 years after we have become Orthodox, we don't see the great numbers of decisions for Christ on the front end that we did back in our parachurch days, because that's all we did. It just isn't very hard to get a college kid to pray a prayer to give his life to Christ. We had them by the thousands. But here I am, all these years later. I love my days in Campus Crusade, but I'm only in touch with a handful of those people (and thank God for those who did go on). But now, operating as an Orthodox parish, while we don't see the front-end numbers, we see an incredibly better rate of the fruit remaining than we did in those parachurch days. So percentage-wise, we're way ahead, though numerically we don't see the volume of those initial decisions. Of course also as Orthodox we tend not to count decisions, we count disciples. Again, you can get a person to pray a prayer, and I'm not the judge of whether that prayer is sincere or not—but what I'm really looking for today is not who started the race, but who's finishing the race. To me that's crucial.

AGAIN: Do you think anything like what happened in the seventies will ever happen again? Do you see any chance for a group of Christians to come alive to Orthodoxy and to pursue it all the way to the finish line?

FPG: I do. I say to people, we've learned how to bring individuals into the Church, we've learned how to bring families into the Church, we've learned how to bring entire non-Orthodox parishes into the Church, we've brought one denomination in (that's ours, the Evangelical Orthodox Church), and I look to the day when we begin to bring other denominations in. But so far that hasn't happened. I was just talking to an Orthodox priest in the Midwest today who had just been invited by a group of traditional pastors within a fairly liberal denomination to come and work with them. They were writing a manifesto to their denomination, saying, "These things have got to change or we're gone." This is happening more and more.

You're probably aware that one entire diocese of the Episcopal Church has pulled out, and two or three others, I'm told, are in the wings ready to pull out. So it may be that before we bring a denomination in, perhaps we can bring in a diocese or some other body, and then work toward the day when an entire denomination will come. A hundred years ago, a lot of people, both in the Episcopal Church and in the Orthodox Church, thought that a natural marriage would be the Episcopal Church in the US with the Orthodox Church. Men like St. Tikhon were at the forefront of this movement. But with the Episcopal Church today moving further and further away from the apostolic faith we read about in the New Testament, probably that dream is more of a nightmare, and it won't happen.

Out there, both within some of these huge denominations and also within the newer communions and the independent churches, there are so many people who are biblically oriented, who are Christ-centered, whose hearts are given toward outreach and help for the poor and so on. These are the people we're picking up today, and I'm very thankful for that, but I really hope there will be again more than one larger body of churches that will come and be a part of the Orthodox Church.

AGAIN: You cited as an example a couple of Episcopal dioceses that are leaving the Episcopal Church. Have these shown any indication that they are seriously considering entering the Orthodox fold?

FPG: I would say not at this point. If I'm correct, they are struggling to find out just exactly what to do. Sometimes they look overseas, for example to Anglican bishops in Africa, as a possible place where they could come and live under their oversight. I have written one of these diocesan bishops who's left and offered to be of help, but to date have not received an answer, which doesn't surprise me. I'll stay available and see if perhaps something doesn't happen down the line.

AGAIN: What would you like to add to this interview? What

final words would you like to say to the contemporary readers of *AGAIN* magazine?

FPG: First, I'd like to say thanks for your support over the years. It's really been gratifying that a magazine that started to serve basically a small group of pilgrims is now reaching out not only to hundreds and hundreds of Orthodox here and throughout the world, but also to a fairly large segment of subscribers who are not yet Orthodox, and we're grateful for that.

Secondly, take heart. God is continuing to bring people into His Holy Church. I would like to see more non-believers come and be converted to Christ within the Orthodox Church—that seems to be picking up, albeit slowly.

Besides that, I would just add one thing. Over the years non-Orthodox people have asked me, as they're considering becoming a part of the Church, do the Orthodox people really mean it? Are they really sold out to this Orthodox faith, or are they simply Orthodox because their parents and grandparents were? Of course that's for each Orthodox Christian to answer for himself or herself. I would say the greatest favor we can do to help those who are not Orthodox is to fully live this spiritual life. Instead of nominal Christians who worship God when it's convenient, we need to be people who pull out all the stops and, as we say at the end of our great litany, "to commit ourselves and each other and all our lives to Christ our God."

More Photos

Peter, age 3, in 1941

Marilyn as a college graduate, 1962

Wedding, 1960

Fr. Peter and Marilyn at their wedding in 1960 (above)
and below in 1990

Above: Family Christmas card, 1971, Memphis, TN. Left to right: Ginger, Terri, Peter, Marilyn holding Heidi, Wendy, Greg.

Below: Thanksgiving 2001, Santa Barbara, CA. Left to right: Terri, Peter Jon, Wendy, Greg, Heidi, Fr. Peter, Marilyn, Ginger.

Above: Fr. Peter at St. Athanasius in Goleta, CA, in May 2009

Below: Fr. Peter's funeral vigil at All Saints' Antiochian Orthodox Church in Bloomington, IN, on July 4, 2012

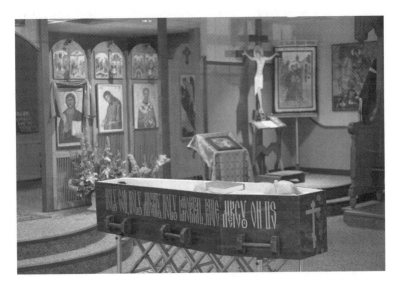

Great-grandson Peter visiting "GeeGee's" grave, 2015

Also by V. Rev. Peter Gillquist

Becoming Orthodox
A Journey to the Ancient Christian Faith

After a long and difficult journey, 2000 weary evangelical Protestants found their way home. This is the story of a handful of courageous men and their congregations who risked stable occupations, security, and the approval of lifelong friends to be obedient to God's call. It is also the story of every believer who is searching for the Church where Christ is Lord and holiness, human responsibility, and the Sovereignty of God are preached.
Paperback, 176 pages, ISBN 978-1-936270-02

available at store.ancientfaith.com

Ancient Faith Publishing hopes you have enjoyed and benefited from this book. The proceeds from the sales of our books only partially cover the costs of operating our nonprofit ministry—which includes both the work of **Ancient Faith Publishing** and the work of **Ancient Faith Radio**. Your financial support makes it possible to continue this ministry both in print and online. Donations are tax-deductible and can be made at www.ancient-faith.com.

To request a catalog of other publications,
please call us at (800) 967-7377 or (219) 728-2216
or log onto our website: **store.ancientfaith.com**

ANCIENT FAITH RADIO

Bringing you Orthodox Christian music, readings,
prayers, teaching, and podcasts 24 hours a day since 2004 at
www.ancientfaith.com